PORTFOLIO

THE CATALOGUE OF CONTEMPORARY PHOTOGRAPHY IN BRITAIN

Number 24 December 1996

Published in June and December by Portfolio Gallery, Photography Workshop (Edinburgh) Limited, 43 Candlemaker Row, Edinburgh EH1 2QB, UK Tel (44) 0131 220 1911 Fax (44) 0131 226 4287

SUBSCRIPTIONS

UNITED KINGDOM
Individuals -
£27 for 4 issues / £15 for 2 issues
Institutions, Libraries and Colleges -
£45 for 4 issues / £25 for 2 issues

EUROPE -
£45 for 4 issues / £25 for 2 issues

WORLDWIDE -
Air £55 for 4 issues / £30 for 2 issues
See form on page 72

DISTRIBUTION

UK Museum and Gallery Bookshops: PORTFOLIO, 43 Candlemaker Row, Edinburgh EH1 2QB, UK Tel (44) 0131 220 1911 Fax (44) 0131 226 4287

UK Retail: Art Data, 12 Bell Industrial Estate, 50 Cunnington Street, London W4 5HB Tel (44) 0181 747 1061 Fax (44) 0181 742 2319

USA, Canada, Europe and Asia: D.A.P./Distributed Art Publishers, Inc. 155 Avenue of the Americas, 2nd Floor, New York 10013 Tel (212) 627 1999 Fax (212) 627 9484

Editor: Gloria Chalmers

Advertising: Catherine Williams

Subscriptions and Distribution: Christine Frew

Design Consultants: Tayburn McIlroy Coates

Typesetting: Patricia Bartie

ISSN 1354-4446

Printed on Consort Royal Satin Manufactured by UK Paper Speciality Papers Division, Donside Mill

Reprographics by Leeds Photo Litho

Printed and bound in England by Jackson-Wilson Printers

THE SCOTTISH ARTS COUNCIL

Cover Detail from Mundus Subterraneus I, 1996, by Calum Colvin

Plates

Essays

Reviews

Photographs:
Calum Colvin Mundus Subterraneus IV, 1996
Gabriel Orozco Until You Find Another Yellow Schwalbe, 1995
Willie Doherty At the End of the Day, 1994 (single screen video installation with sound)

Calum Colvin
Pseudologica Fantastica

Mundus Subterraneus III, 1996

Mundus Subterraneus I, 1996 *(opposite)*

MUNDUS SUBTERR

Detail from Untitled - Triptychs 1, 2, 3 & 4, 1996 *(and overleaf)*

Mundus Subterraneus IX, 1996

Mundus Subterraneus XI, 1996 *(opposite)*

Gabriel Orozco

Sandball and Chair 1, 1995

Ball on Water, 1994 *(opposite)*

Empty Shoe Box, 1993

Hose, 1995 *(opposite)*

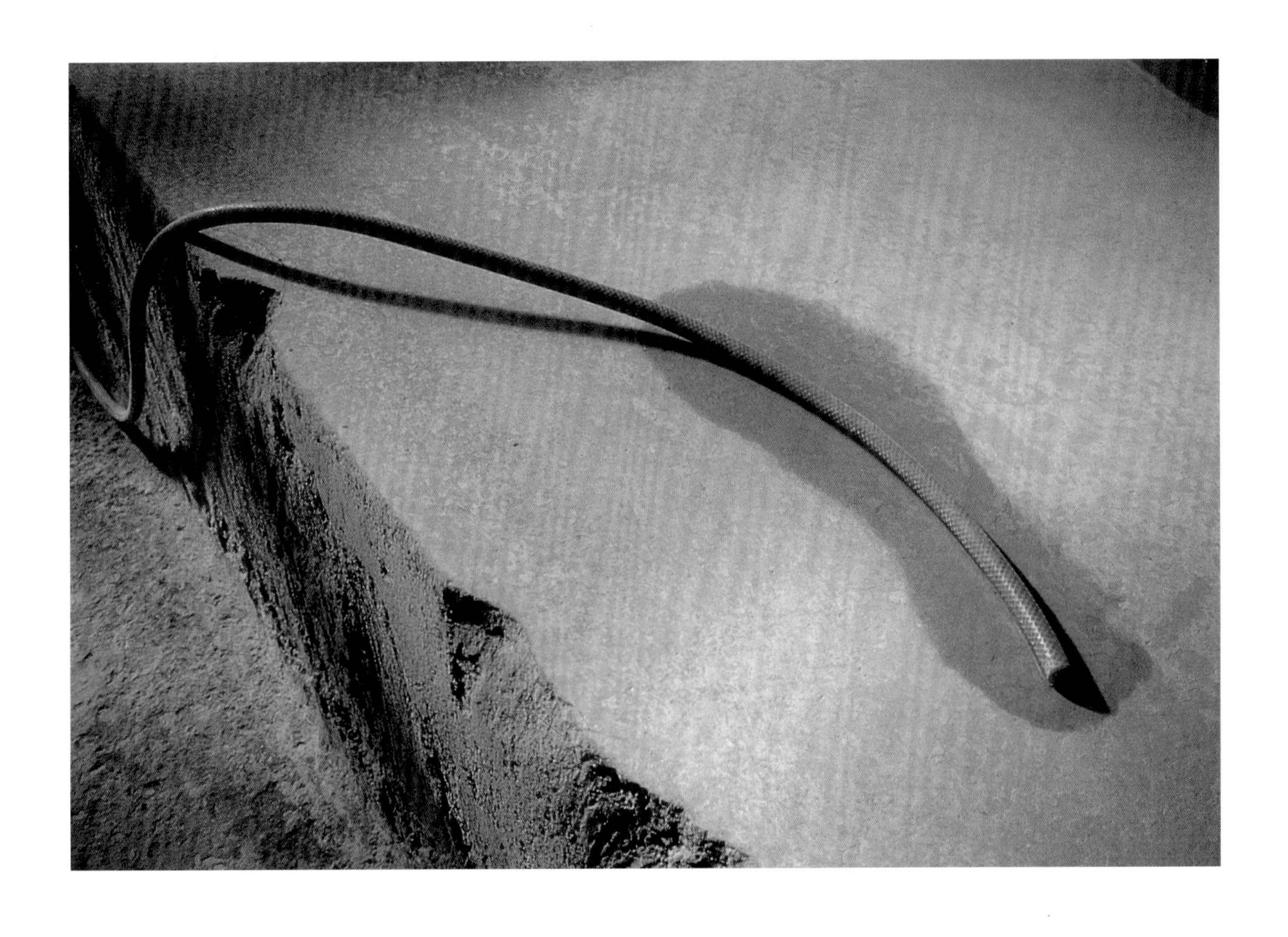

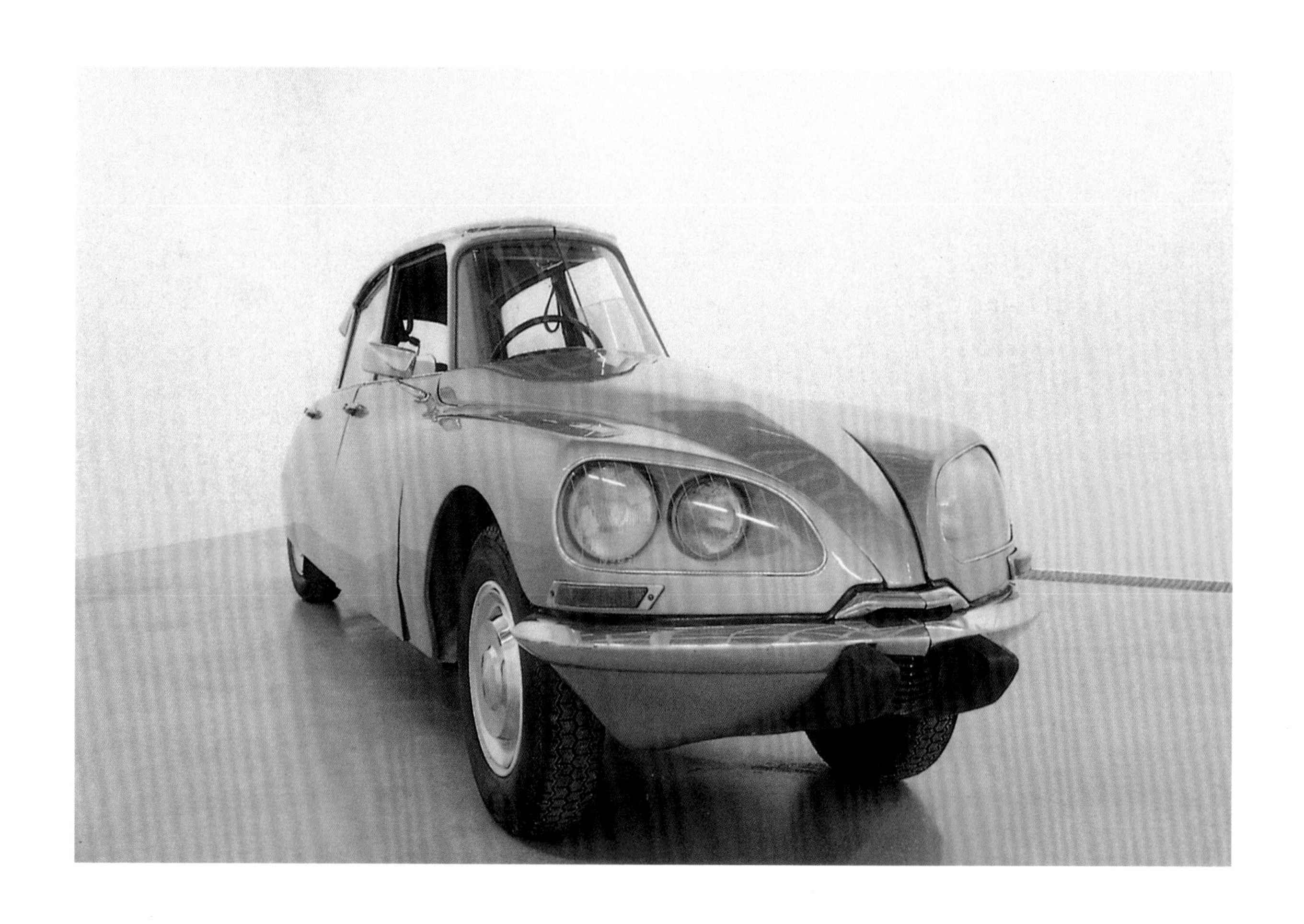

La DS, 1993

Green Ball, 1995 *(opposite)*

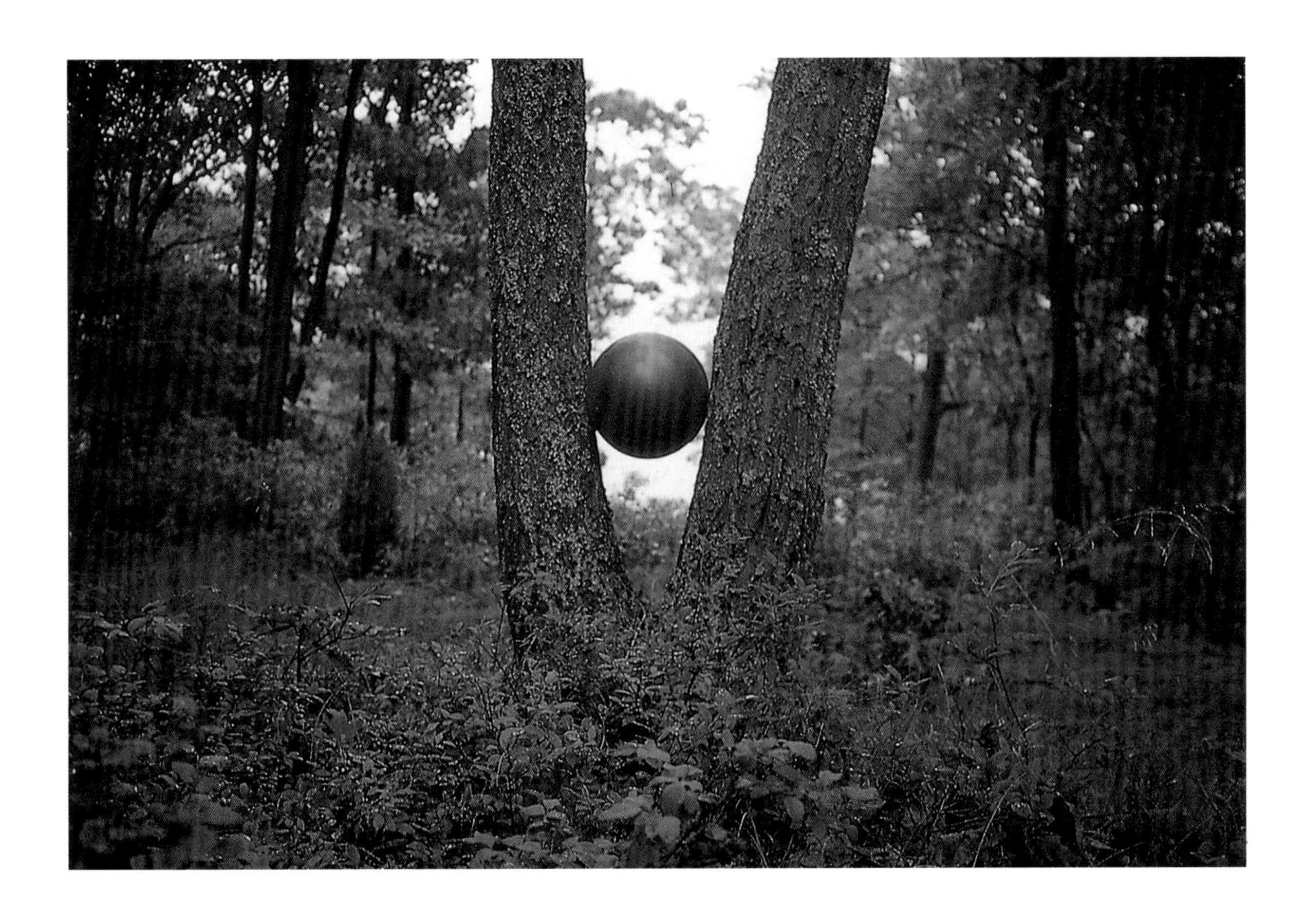

John Goto
The Framer's Collection

BLACKMORE TAILORS
Ulah & Rose
CINEMA
Roberto Rossellini's PAISA
Roberto Rossellini's PAISA
OPTICAL Co 167

Susan Trangmar
Exposures

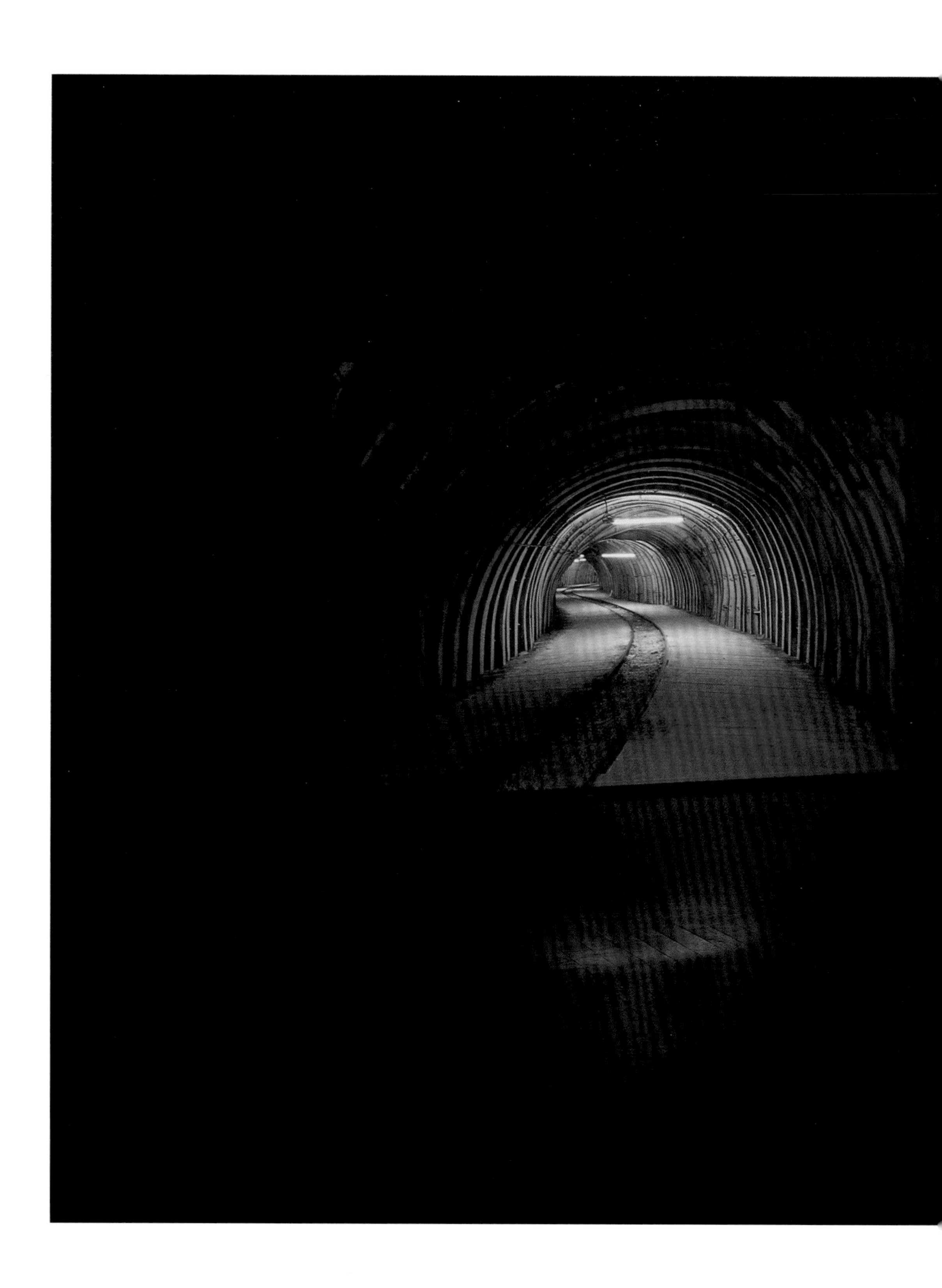

Exposures projection installation, 1996

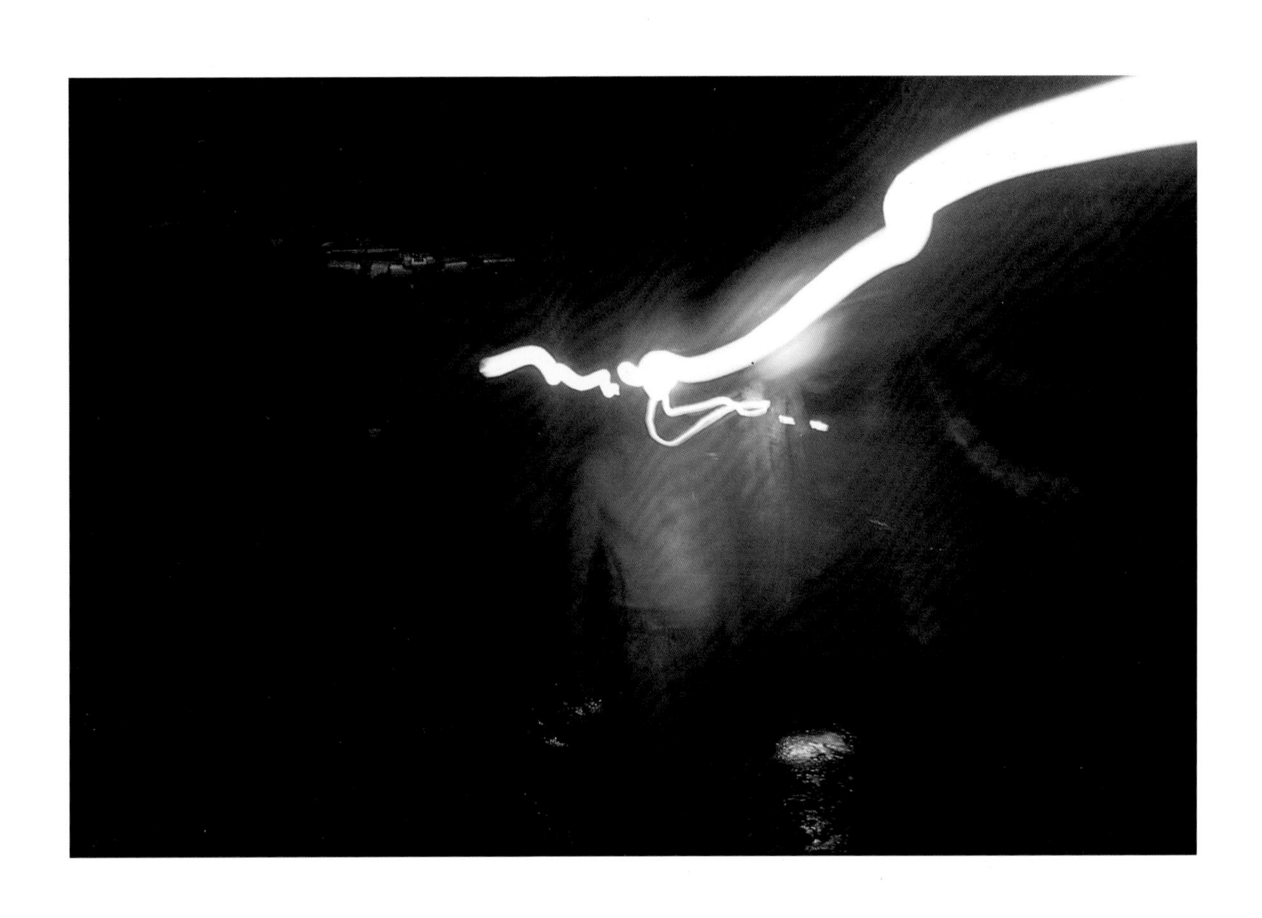

Exposures 1996 detail *(above and opposite)*

Exposures 1996 detail *(above and opposite)*

Willie Doherty
No Smoke Without Fire

Bullet Holes, 1995

Minor Incident 2, 1994 *(opposite)*

Factory (Reconstruction), 1995

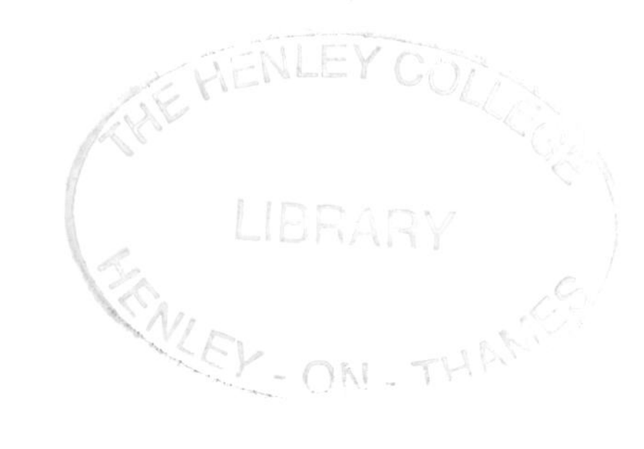

Richard Billingham

Ray's a Laugh

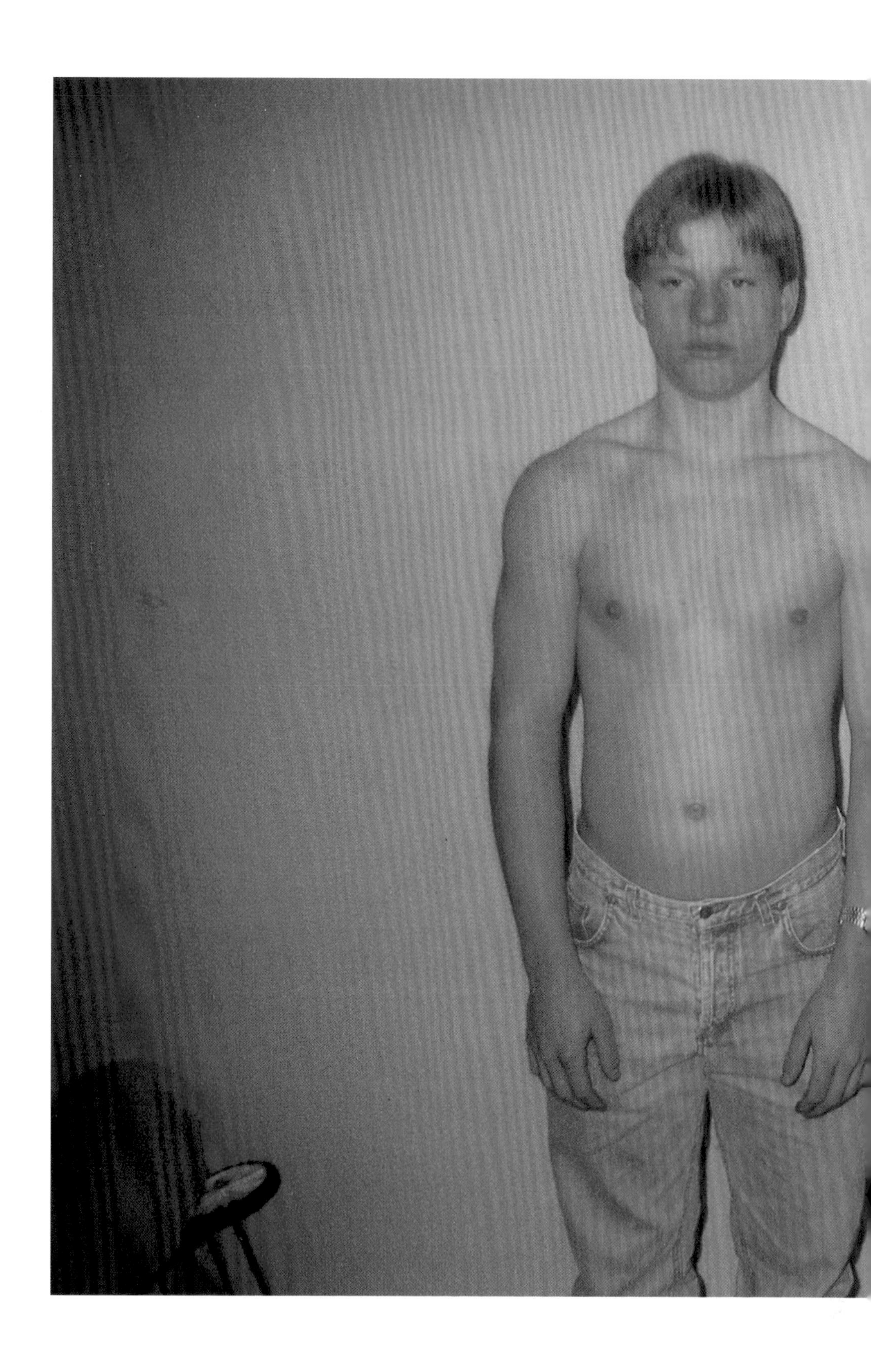

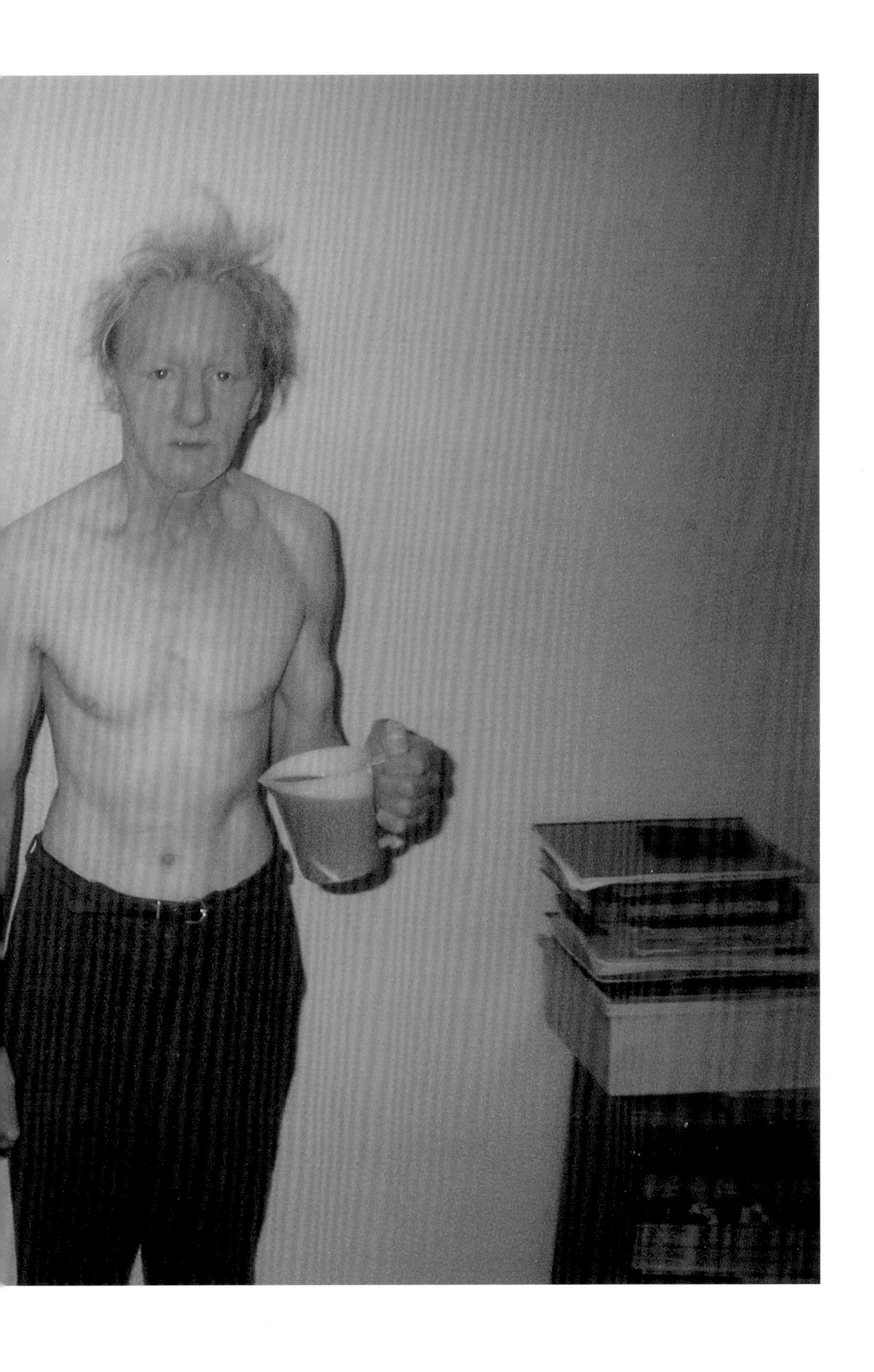

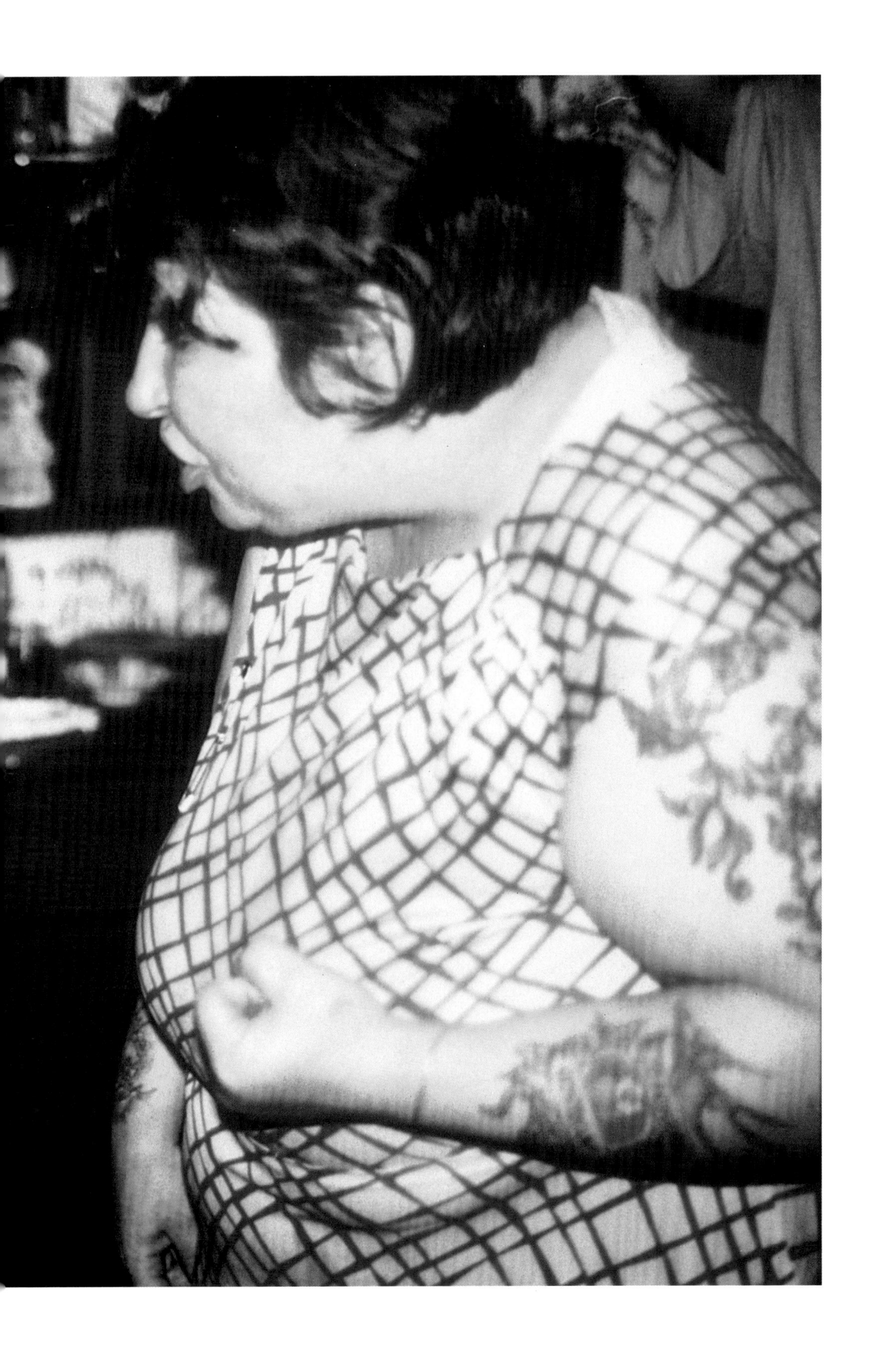

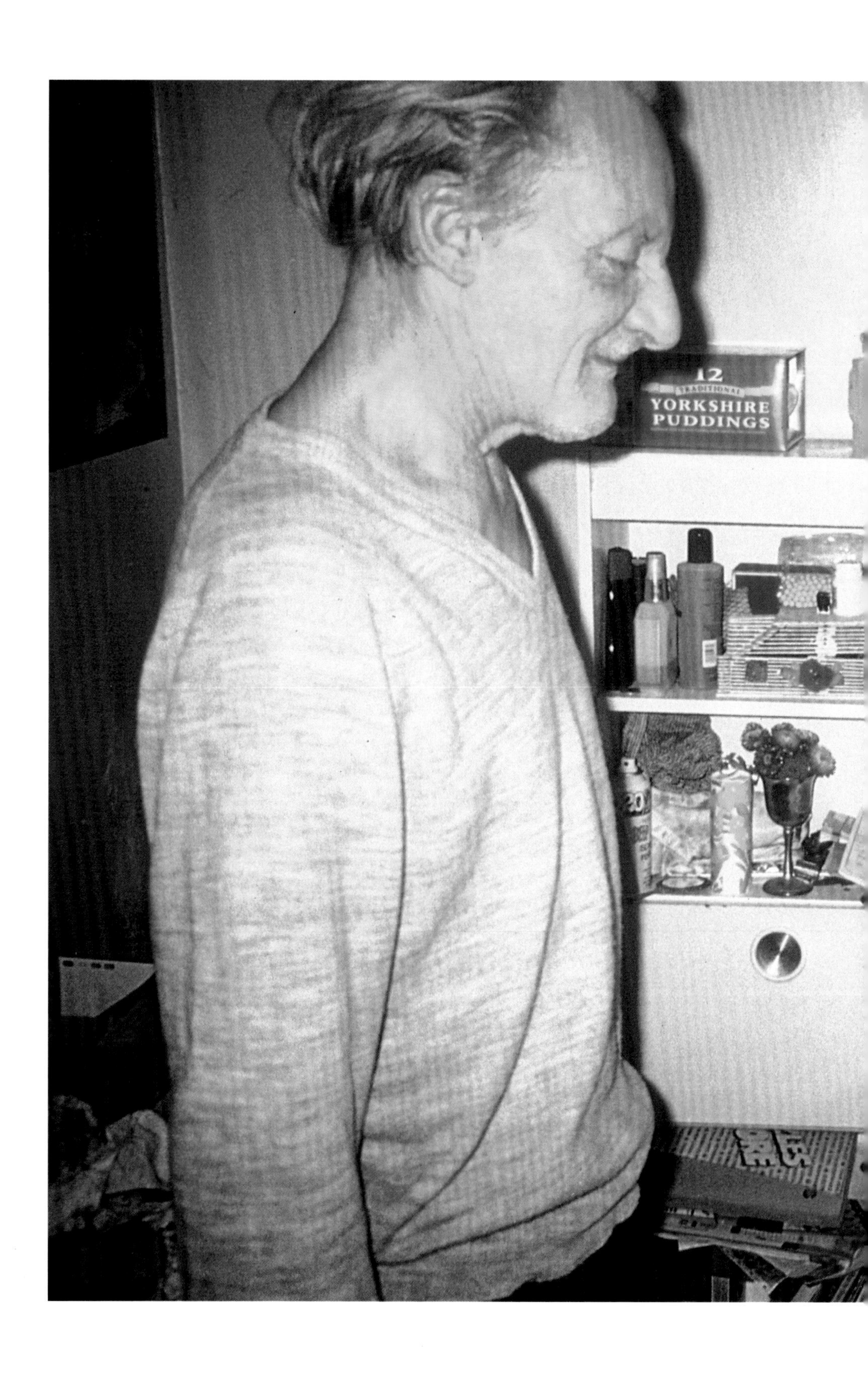
12
TRADITIONAL
YORKSHIRE
PUDDINGS

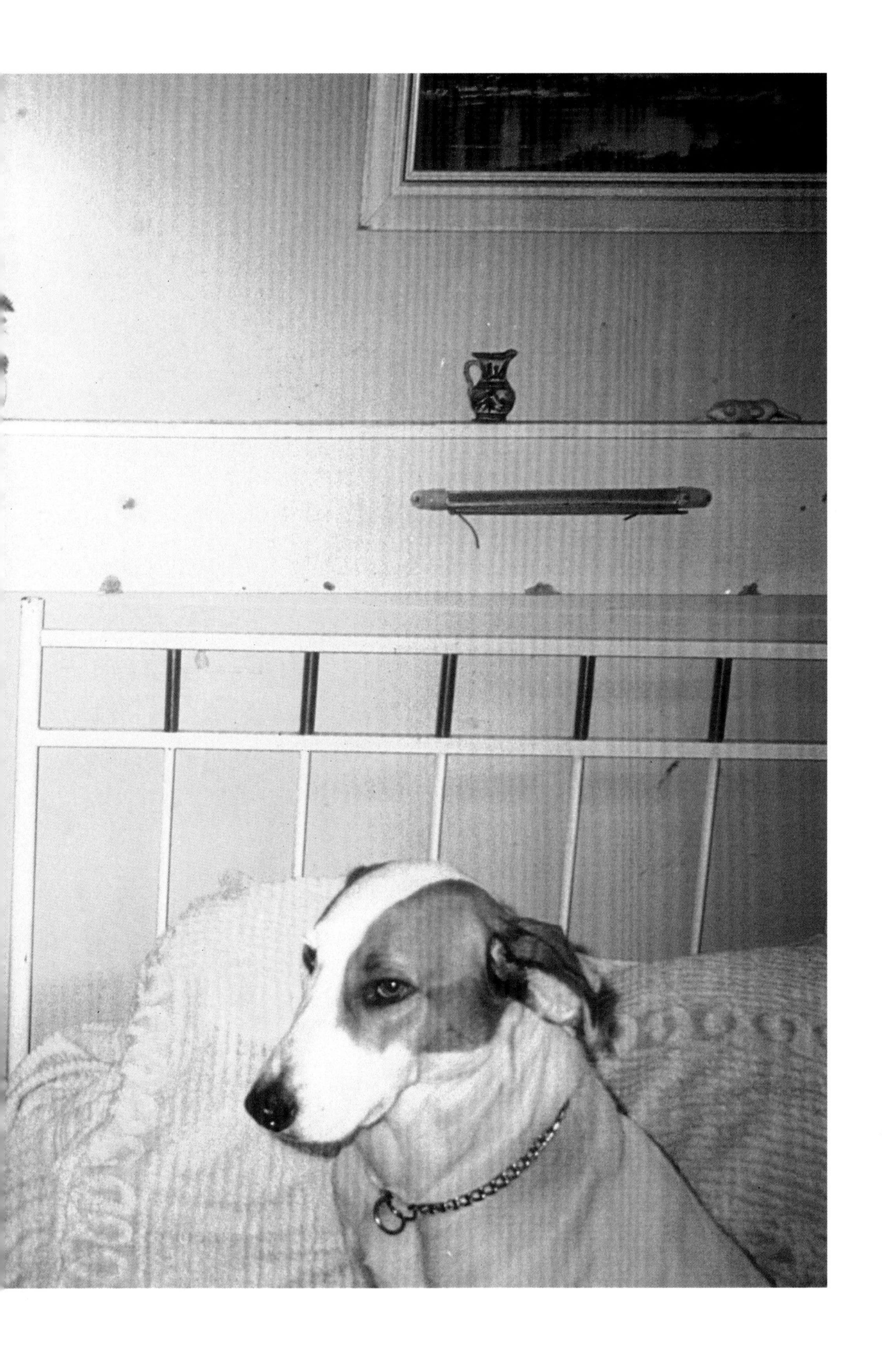

Jim Mooney
Where Absence Glows Visible

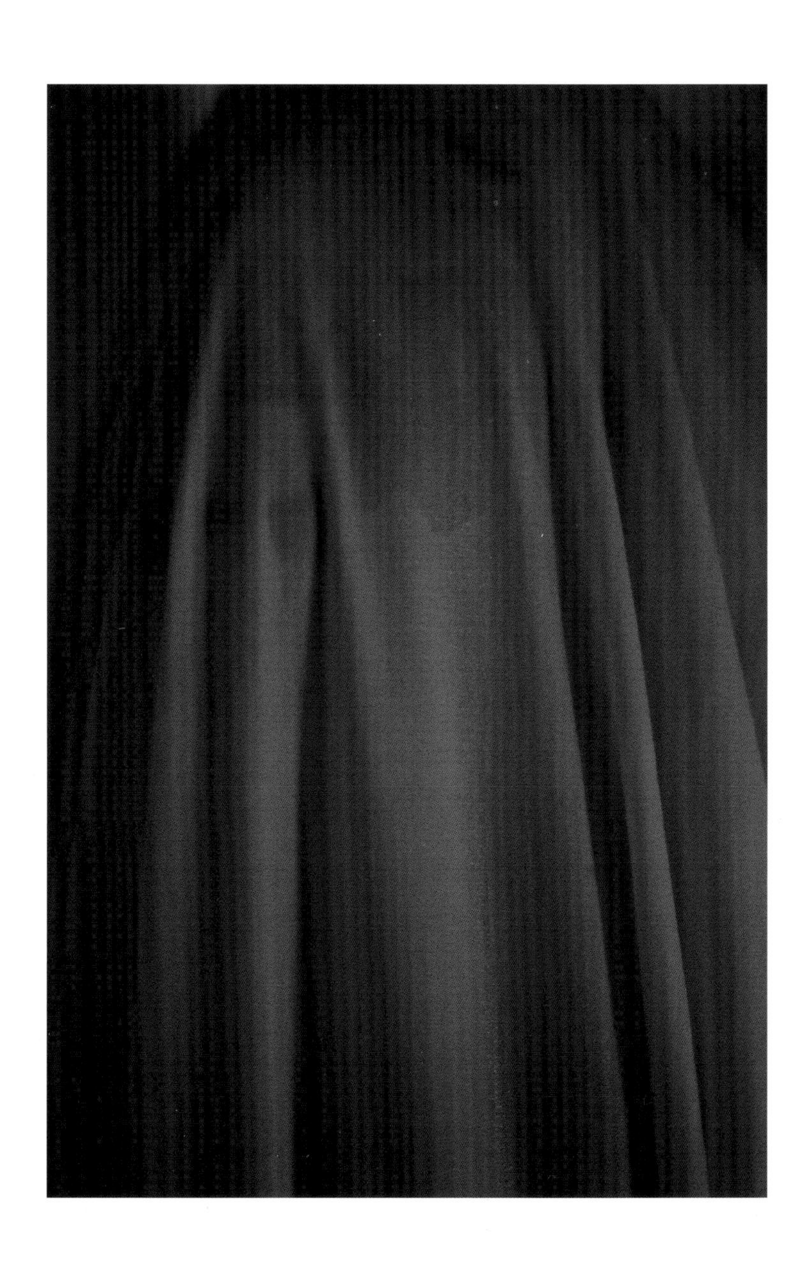

From the Shroud series, 1996

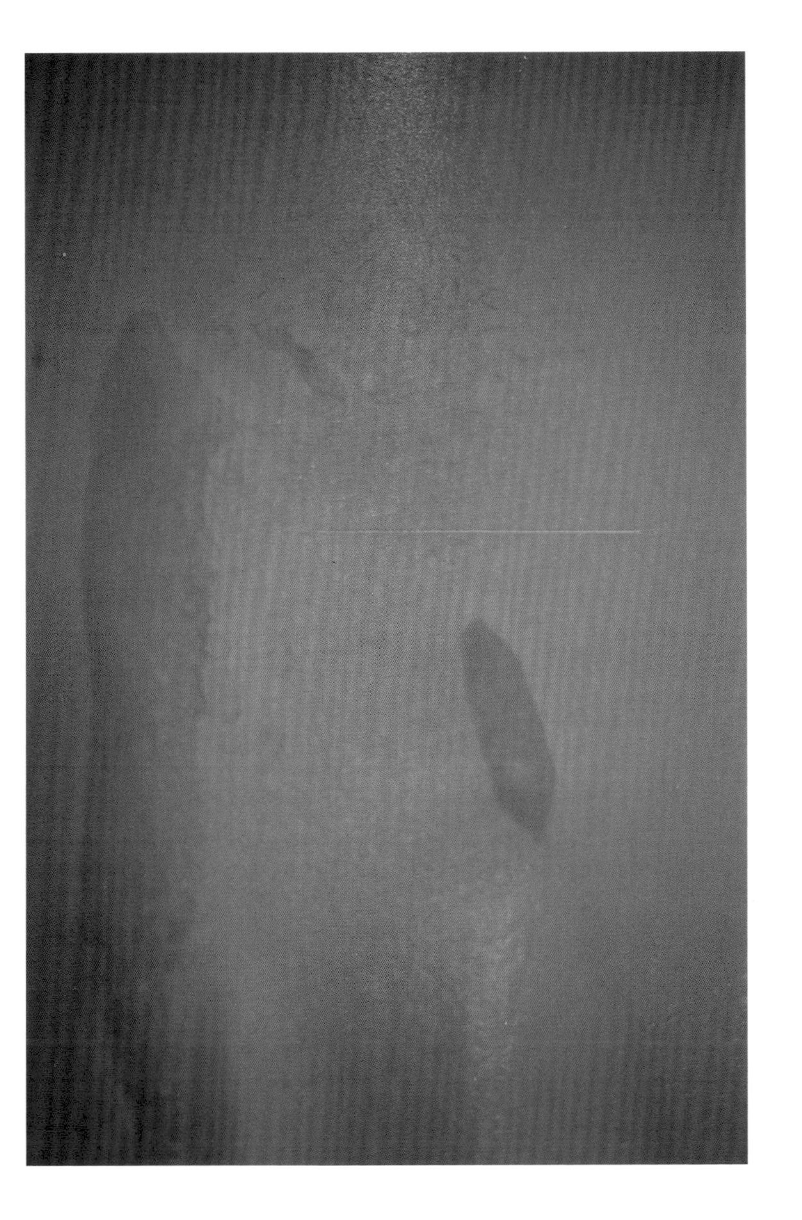

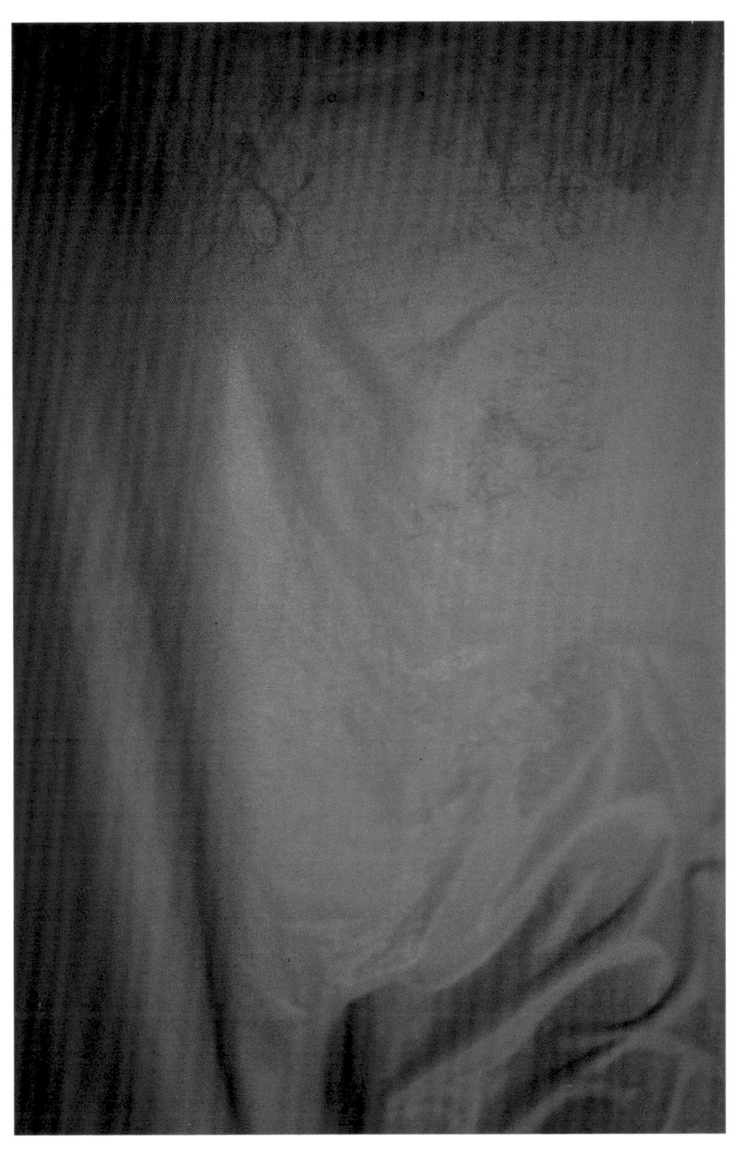

Face to Face, 1995

Scotoma, 1995 *(opposite)*

Annette Heyer
Portfolio

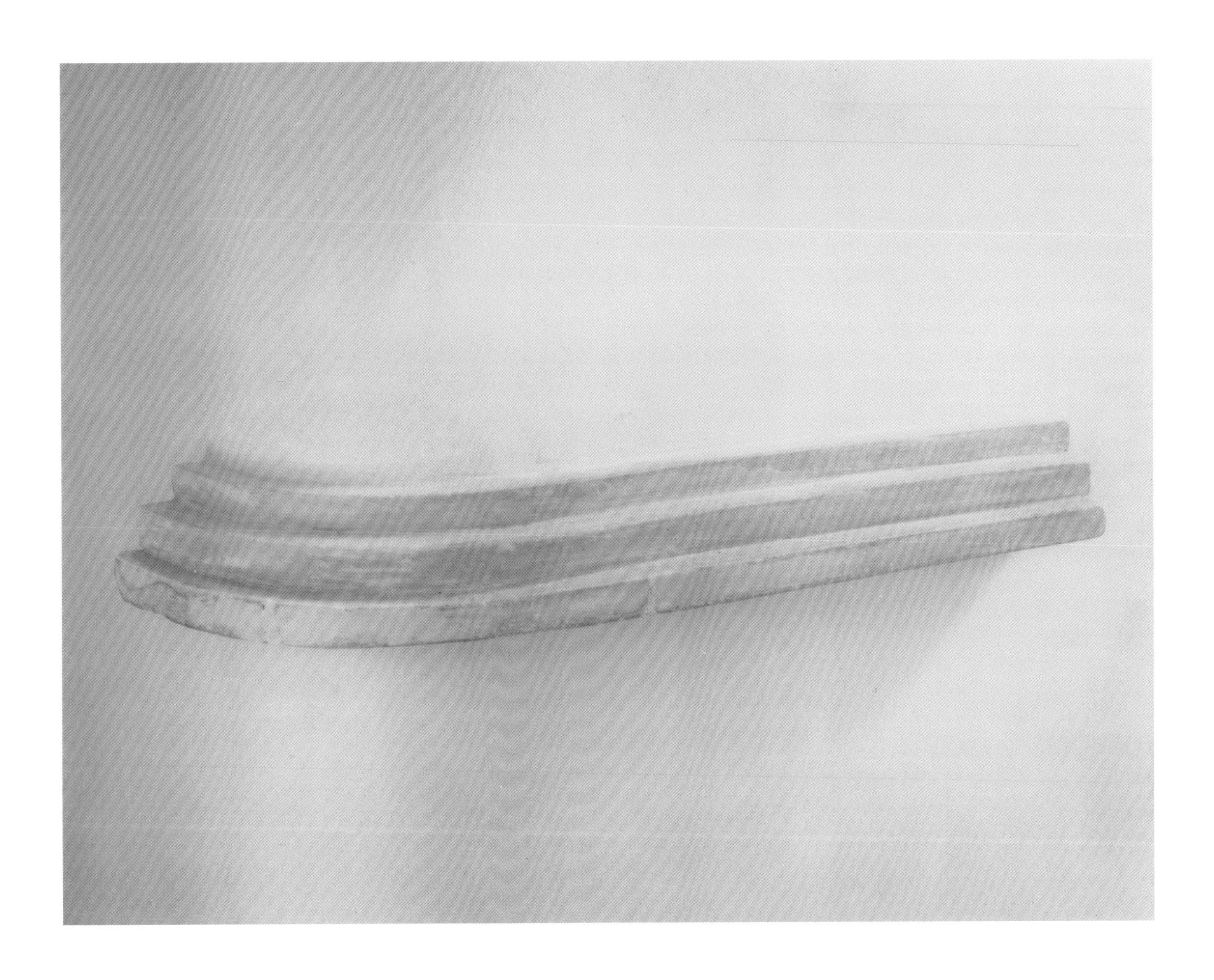

Corridor, 1996

Corner, 1996 *(opposite)*

Robert Mapplethorpe

Calla Lily, 1988

Ajitto, 1981 *(opposite)*

Lisa Lyon, 1982

Catalogue

CALUM COLVIN

All works are cibachrome prints

Mundus Subterraneus III, 1996
115 x 147 cm

Mundus Subterraneus I, 1996
147 x 115 cm

Untitled - Triptychs 1, 2, 3 & 4
64.5 cm x 17.26 metres

Mundus Subterraneus IX, 1996
115 x 143 cm

Mundus Subterraneus XI, 1996
115 x 143 cm

Courtesy the Artist

GABRIEL OROZCO

Sandball and Chair 1, 1995
Cibachrome print 16 x 20 inches

Ball on Water, 1994
Cibachrome print 16 x 20 inches

Empty Shoe Box, 1993
Cibachrome print 9 x 13.25 inches

Hose, 1995
Cibachrome print 16 x 20 inches

La DS, 1993
Sutured car: metal, leather, coated fabric
140 x 480 x 114cm

Green Ball, 1995
Cibachrome print 16 x 20 inches

Courtesy of Marian Goodman Gallery, New York and the Institute of Contemporary Arts, London

JOHN GOTO

All works are C-type colour prints. Three shown from a series of six.

Installation View I
46 x 76 inches

Installation View II
46 x 76 inches

Installation View III
46 x 76 inches

Courtesy the Artist

SUSAN TRANGMAR

Exposures projection installation, Angel Row Gallery, Nottingham, 1996

Exposures (details), 1996

Courtesy the Artist

WILLIE DOHERTY

Bullet Holes, 1995
Cibachrome on aluminium
76 x 102 cm

Minor Incident 2, 1994
Cibachrome on aluminium
76 x 102 cm

Factory (Reconstruction), 1995
Single monitor video installation
Dimensions variable

Courtesy Matt's Gallery, London

RICHARD BILLINGHAM

All works are editioned chromogenic prints

Pages 32, 33
105 x 158 cm

Pages 34, 35
80 x 120 cm

Pages 36, 37
80 x 120 cm

Courtesy Anthony Reynolds Gallery, London, and the National Museum of Photography, Film and Television, Bradford

JIM MOONEY

Shroud, 1996
Three cibachrome prints from a series of ten works
Each 142 x 92 cm

Face to Face, 1995
Black-and-white photographic installation
183 x 427 cm

Scotoma, 1995
Black-and-white photographic installation
Dimensions variable

Courtesy the Artist

ANNETTE HEYER

Corridor, 1996
Gelatin silver print
100 x 140 cm

Corner, 1996
Gelatin silver print
140 x 100 cm

Courtesy the Artist

ROBERT MAPPLETHORPE

Calla Lily,1988
Gelatin silver print, 60 x 50 cm

Ajitto, 1981
Gelatin silver print, 100 x 76 cm

Lisa Lyon, 1982
Gelatin silver print, 50 x 40 cm

Courtesy the Hayward Gallery, London

Acknowledgements

Works in Calum Colvin's **Pseudologica Fantastica** were output onto transparency and printed by **Genex Imaging, London**, as cibachrome prints.

John Goto acknowledges the support of **Oxford Brookes University** and **Stoneleigh Photographic Services** of Leamington Spa.

Susan Trangmar's **Exposures** installation was shown at Angel Row Gallery, Nottingham, 21 May - 22 June 1996. Photograph by Edward Woodman.

Willie Doherty's works from **No Smoke Without Fire** are reproduced by permission of Matt's Gallery, London.

A Package Flight to the Land of the Dead

Calum Colvin's Pseudologica Fantastica

DAVID ALAN MELLOR

HOLIDAYS FROM HELL and holidays *to* hell. In Calum Colvin's new series of digitally generated photographs, **Pseudologica Fantastica**, Spanish tourist hotel corridors and crowded beachscapes have liquified into quicksilver ribbons of madness. Here, holiday memories and siesta intervals fly straight back to purgatory. Colvin's narrative commences with the banal - the scenography of the Great British package holiday - which then swoops into an endless ruin. His *Triptychs 1* and *2* trace, like an unrolled scroll, a racing body of desire made up of sunbathers. This becomes a twister of deformed images, a tornado of whirling and sucking which forcefully constricts itself through architectonic apertures in a sort of peristaltic movement, before returning, like the genie lured back into its flask. It goes back into a yellow dial from the timing mechanism for central heating - a regulator of heat, a fantastic object following in the footsteps of Picabia and Duchamp's mechanical analogues for desire. Yet at the end of these city triptychs the ribbon of dreams is seen again, but not as a single flowing wave of squeezed images. Now it is infinitely slowed down, separated as single flipped photos, revenants from the Spanish holiday. They stir and fly listlessly through the frames of the mansions of the dead, like Plato's uncorrupted soul on a visit. In the city of the dead, memory is encoded in and on stone: the monumental pylons that compose Colvin's subterranean world have disquieting vestiges of events still adhering to them - scorch marks in the shape of human silhouettes and barnacle forms that have traded places with the rocks from the Spanish beach Happy-Snaps.

A certain disgust with the corporeal body (in the age of the virtual) runs at all levels through *Pseudologica Fantastica.* Examples within the series include the UV-damaged, but still tanning humans on the beach: a spectacle, Colvin has said, resembling 'a combination of *Bladerunner* and Blackpool'[1] - the bizarre and the banal together. There is the burnt and shattered hand, as if left on the Basra road in March 1991; the disinterred skull; and the miller's doomed coupling with the siren in *Mundus Subterraneus VI-VIII,* which ends in disaster amidst chaotic waves.

Colvin's newest work has been mainly inspired by the 17th century Jesuit, Athanasius Kircher. His book, *The Subterranean World,* was a philippic, a denunciation of the alchemist's culture - from the point of view of an ex-alchemist - presenting them as 'a congregation of knaves and impostors'[2]. Kircher was disillusioned and angry at the failure of the 'Great Work' of transmuting the base world: the alchemical project was revealed by him as delusory. Colvin's cautionary version of Kircher's subterranean world is titled **Pseudologica Fantastica** and it, in turn, addresses a prevalent folly of our time. Just as Kircher's *Subterranean World* took aim at alchemy, Colvin's contemporary 'popular delusion' is an apocalypticism of the image. His landscapes rebuke the bizarre, the morphed and the Face on Mars, and puts them in a sobered, Dante-esque setting.

Pseudologica Fantastica disinters and unwinds an ascetic set of grave commentaries by Colvin on our contemporary mortified distractions. The precedent is *Urne Buriall,* written by another 17th century polymath, Sir Thomas Browne, another cataloguer of bizarre popular delusions, in his *Pseudodoxia Epidemica.* Browne began his voyage into the customs of the underworld with a paradoxical turn of speech and representation: 'In the deep discovery of the Subterranean world, a shallow part would satisfie some enquirers...'[3] Colvin's comedy narrative of the miller's flying machine is perched upon a watery horizon, while Browne named water as 'the smartest grave'[4]: he nominated two principal forms of 'corporal dissolution... simple inhumation and burning'[5]. In Colvin's 'subterranean world' flames leap up as *Ignis Fatuus* in the city of the dead. Separately, he has presented the scene of burning with bony claws, scorched paper and rubble. Fiery particles are driven by the imperative to transform the corpse to avoid 'contagion and pollution'. In *Triptych 3* flames leap up in the lair of horrors, with hot red plastic zombies and the agonised Hellenistic heads that we last saw in Colvin's repertory in his *Brief Encounter* version of Leighten's *Athlete Wrestling with a Python,* in 1990.

This is a world of imperial evolutionary growths that have been dismantled, of vectors and drives which have petered out and run into the desert, returning to inert, stony matter - a devolution from higher to lower. Either the disinterred skull of Colvin's *Mundus Subterraneus* is already embalmed, with its brains replaced by curved and chambered photographs of the beach and corridors of Lloret de Mar, or it is a relic of failed inhumation, along with the blasted hand. Browne was writing in 1658 in the wake of the discovery, at Walsingham, of forty to fifty Romano-British burial urns containing '...ribs, jaws, thigh bones and teeth'.[6] This is what composes the techno-skull in *Mundus Subterraneus I,* an antler-jawed relic which has fallen into his hands, the hands of an inveterate constructor of tabernacles and oracular situations since his earliest temple-like contrivances in works such as *Cenotaph* (1987), *The Temptation of St Anthony* (1989), and *Brief Encounter* (1990).

In this new work there is a reversal of expectations about the legibility and substantiality of different forms of imaging; his terminal and interminable beaches, actual and recorded on film, become de-realised by pixillation and digitisation - turned into teardrop reliquaries of our desired images of consumer leisure. Colvin appears to take a posture of mistrust to these scenes of photo-generated representation, a form of scepticism which mortifies the instruments of photography through metamorphosis: the skull as a camera and a photographer's tripod as the forearm support of a dead hand.

The scenography of a wasteland, populated with corpses and menacing relics that have not yet returned to cycles of decomposition, has its prompts in T. S. Eliot. 'What are the roots that clutch, what branches grow / Out of this stony rubbish?...(T. S. Eliot, *The Waste Land,* lines 19-20). 'That corpse you planted last year in your garden / Has it begun to sprout?... with nails he'll dig it up again' (lines 71, 75). The obtrusive return of dead organic matter is thematised by the rise of an ashen rose in the sky in *Mundus Subterraneus IX,* resembling one of David Hiscock's post-volcanic bouquets. This blighting effect should be taken together with the blasted photographic flesh found in tatters at the end of the reach of the dead hand. In *Mundus Subterraneus V,* Colvin's Scottish rider has been assimilated into the persona of the Angel of Death, but is still thrown by something macabre and essentially base which is stirring from the earth. The rider and horse are suspended between two subterranean worlds with no prospect of progress or direction home, since they are caught in the baleful gaze of that primal ancestor of *homo sapiens,* the ape. He emerges from the gritty soil above and below, and, in a derisory signal, he sticks his tongue out at the triumphal rider.

With Colvin, the means of producing a photographic or screened and scanned image arises directly from the ravaged but technologically augmented body. For example, the camera bellows protruding from the spinal column in *Mundus Subterraneus II* projects a central nervous system with a capacity to generate pictures like Max Ernst's levitated female statue in *La Femme Cent Têtes* (1929)[7], which exposes 'the means of this illusion's production'.[8] Into the spine of *Mundus Subterraneus II* are pouring a reservoir of images from a floating globe. These photo-images are of deserted beaches and sunset-lit gateways - pictures purged of the sordid proximities of bodies found in his Lloret de Mar beach photos. The scenes are of a purified and atmospherically charged home - the streets and beach of Colvin's Edinburgh suburb of Portobello - and they are smokily decanted like an alchemic liquor flowing into the projector. Another such melding of parts comes with the passage from the Angel of Death's feathered wings to the ectoplasmic ribbon of leisure dreams and nightmares, in *Mundus Subterraneus V.*

Mundus Subterraneus IV carries questing, sporting and erotic narrative fragments that are present on the weathered and stained TV screens broadcasting them into the barren world, like the grey disused PC monitors in *Ars Magna.* The central screen in *Mundus Subterraneus IV* reads 'The End', blazoned across an eerie electronically-transmitted version of the enclosed Spanish hotel corridor. That corridor vanishing point, a repeated place of reverie for the eye amidst the crowded sequence of bodies, becomes a point of ingress, doubled by those split monumental masonry blocks of the town of the dead, through which the ribbon of images flow. The image arises from another bizarre metaphor of an unburied body part - a group of rigidly inflated plastic toy hearts, lying on beds of candy-floss, which are grounded forever in the subterranean world.

1. Calum Colvin to the author, 12 October 1996, York.
2. C. McKay, *Extraordinary Popular Delusions and the Madness of Crowds*, 1995, Wordsworth, Hertfordshire. p.213
3 Ed. Sir Geoffrey Keynes, *Sir Thomas Browne/Selected Writings*, Faber and Faber, London, 1970, p.110.
4. Op. cit. p.119.
5. Op. cit. p.120.
5. Op. cit. p.124.
7. Reproduced by R. Krauss, 'The Im/Pulse to See', ed. H. Foster, *Vision and Visuality,* Bay Press, 1988, p.56.
8. Krauss, op. cit. p.55.

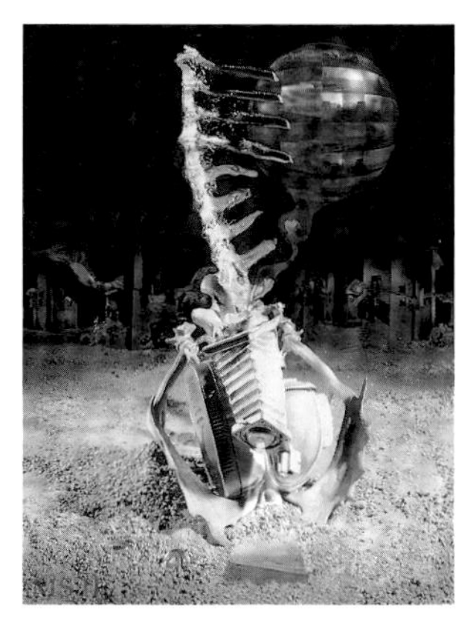

MUNDUS SUBTERRANEUS II, 1996

MUNDUS SUBTERRANEUS V, 1996

Memos for the Present Moment

Gabriel Orozco

DAVID WARD

Whenever humanity seems condemned to heaviness, I think I should fly like Perseus into a different space. I don't mean escaping into dreams or into the irrational. I mean that I have to change my approach, look at the world from a different perspective, with a different logic and with fresh methods of cognition and verification. The images of lightness that I seek should not fade away like dreams dissolved by the realities of the present and future.......

Italo Calvino[1]

ONE MID-SUMMER AFTERNOON in London, I walked with H. towards St. James's, passing down through the cool air of Burlington Arcade to the now empty building of a once grandiose 19th century gentleman's club. Entering a set of elaborately decorated reception rooms I heard the strike of a billiard cue and ball.

In the centre of the room stood an oval, green baize billiard table. Leaning over its curved rim a man followed the shot through and stood back as a red ball flew over the side cushion and left the table in a clear arc of ascent into the air. The ball stopped in mid-air and seemed to hover for one astonishing moment before swooping back again. Flying past the player's ear the ball performed a second shining hover. My involuntary cry of amazement was not diminished by the sudden rationalisation of that first moment of flight, when laws of gravity were magically defied before my eyes. I realised that the ball was swinging by an almost invisible thread, suspended from the ceiling.

This was one of a series of works by Gabriel Orozco, each with the theme of a ball game, in the site of *Empty Club*, his Artangel project for London.

In early autumn, I walked with C. through late-season tourists, from Piccadilly Circus (just a few streets away from the *Empty Club*) across Pall Mall, past the gilded goddess of the Athenaeum Club and past the humming pink ice-cream van to descend the steps to the Mall and the ICA Galleries. Outside, roller-blading children were teaching themselves to skate in circles. Inside the gallery, Gabriel Orozco's *Four Bicycles (There is Always One Direction)* performed its own spin on the floor - somewhere between the skating outside and cycling acrobats of the Chinese State Circus - a giddy metaphor perhaps for the *precarious status of the sculptural object.* [2]

The vehicle, as means and metaphor of mobility, finds an exquisite, silver surfaced, attenuated design form in the car body of the Citroen DS - 'goddess' (déesse) - that became Orozco's work *La DS*, after being salvaged from a derelict state. By cutting and welding, the body of the car is re-formed, accentuating both its fabulous objecthood and the mythologising effect of its gendered name. In 1957, when this car first appeared in France, Roland Barthes wrote in *Mythologies*, 'In the exhibition halls, the car on show is explored with an intense, amorous studiousness: it is the great tactile phase of discovery, the moment when visual wonder is about to receive the reasoned assault of touch (for touch is the most demystifying of all senses, unlike sight, which is the most magical).' [3]

In contrast to the streamlines of *La Ds, Yielding Stone* is a lumpen and intensely tactile corporeal ball - of Orozco's own body weight of plasticine - that also irresistibly attracts inquisitive touches. Rolled around city streets, this inert yet receptive body of matter is imprinted and marked by traces of everything in its path.

This 'body of experience' is an analogue for Orozco's own mobility, in the world and within his own practice, that generates works which engage both with their physical, social and cultural contexts and with the sites of our own experience. Consistent themes emerged in the exhibitions in London, where polarised worlds of private privileged spaces and popular public realms inhabit the same metropolitan sphere. Passage through city streets, patterns of circulation, the distribution of recurring spherical bodies, indicators of cultural and social difference, and a vital sense of affinity and recognition - by which I mean mutually acknowledged experience and feeling - appear repeatedly in Orozco's work. It is in the connectedness between his objects and photographs that processes and relationships move - agencies passing unpredictably, back and forth - fluid in their interactions between imagination, delight and the sometimes blunt instrument of the everyday.

In 1985, Italo Calvino, looking towards the future, began *Six Memos for the Next Millennium,* identifying six qualities as vital to the future of literature: *Lightness, Quickness, Exactitude, Visibility, Multiplicity* and *Consistency*. Calvino did not live to see the era to which he was speaking but his 'memos' remain as reminders and gifts, addressed to the future that we now approach and that is rapidly becoming our present.

There is certainly a sense in which Calvino's values seem to provide an appropriate vocabulary to describe qualities of Orozco's work, and I will talk about lightness in particular. But in addition, the photographs function in a similar way to the memo - *a note to help the memory, note of something to be borne in mind.*

If Calvino's 'Memos' are addressed to the future, then Orozco's photographs are 'Memos for the Present', addressing the continuing moment, drawing attention to our experience of the present and it is here that their vivacity, their resistance, their humour and their humaneness lies.

Transitory and mutable materials and conditions, ephemeral states of sleep, liquid and reflectivity, emerge as recurring poetic and often poignant presences within the photographs that record an intensely, though not purely, phenomenological and material register of the world. And lightness, in many of its aspects, is a significant characteristic of those presences.

Lightness is an especially relative, mercurial quality. In Orozco's work the value of lightness appears, as we have seen, as a suspension of gravity, as gyroscopic momentum, as cyclical or centrifugal motion.

Lightness also appears as an essential condition of surfaces. Barthes wrote of the Citroen DS that: 'As for the material itself, it is certain that it promotes a taste for lightness in its magical sense.' Surfaceness and lightness converge in the photograph *Ball on Water* in which the buoyant body of a pearlescent sphere floats in a sky that is itself a sparkling reflection on the moving surface of water. Water vapour condenses and evaporates as a misty haze on shining black lacquer in *Breath on Piano*. This is what we do before we polish, renew, a surface - we get up close and breathe upon it. Breathe life onto it. Meanings of wind, breath and spirit combine in the Greek word *pneûma*, just as breath and spirit coalesce in the Hebrew *Ruach*. Like breath upon the skin, this is perhaps the lightest of all possible forms of physical touch that we can bestow or receive from another. The felicitous image of a green plastic ball lightly lodged in the fork of a tree - *Green Ball* - pictures *something stopped in flight* through air. Held still, yet simply startling, this is also just what we might describe a photograph to be.

Lightness appears too as a capricious light-heartedness, without a hint of irony. Which is not to say that this wit lacks critical weight. There is gravity beneath the surface, just as Calvino remarked that he did not devalue weight, he just had more to say about lightness. This is particularly evident in Orozco's market-stall interventions. Humourous images might result from the re-positioning of produce and packages. Perplexed cat's eyes gaze out from verdant green darkness as a result of placing pet food cans amongst watermelons. Yet this modest, mischievous gesture is part of one of Orozco's most consistent and critical strategies - the transformation of possible meaning through the often inconspicuous yet telling alteration of existing patterns of organisation. Seemingly slight shifts within existing orders nevertheless speak of commodity distribution and economy - subtle registers of the passage of an itinerant artist, roving through visual, social and cultural territories of significant difference.[4]

LA DS, 1993

In Berlin, Orozco circulated city streets on his motorcycle, a yellow Schwalbe, seeking out similar parked machines and photographing his own Schwalbe next to its familiar. The resulting serial work of 40 photographs, *Until You Find Another Yellow Schwalbe*, is organised as a 'cycle' of doubling. But the liaisons which form this work, quite literally take off when, after each fleeting encounter, Orozco left notes to the absent owners, inviting them to a party, held in the car park of the National Gallery to bring together these otherwise estranged owners of a yellow Schwalbe - which translates as Swallow, the migratory bird, always on the wing.

As I write this I am travelling north on a train, turning the pages of Orozco's jewel-like book work containing over 100 photographs.[5] I find myself gazing at a photograph of water drops against the light as they cling to the underside of a window, waiting to fall. A finger tip makes contact with one droplet, surface tension forming a tiny, spherical, lens-like focus of light, held by the lightest touch, a delicate contact delaying a simple act of gravity - a pause, a 'Memo for the Present Moment'. I look up to find it has begun to rain outside.

SAND ON TABLE, 1992

Think what it would be to have a work conceived from outside the ***self****, a work that would let us escape the limited perspective of the individual ego, not only to enter into selves like our own but to give speech to that which has no language, to the bird perching on the edge of the gutter, to the tree in spring and the tree in fall, to stone, to cement, to plastic....*[6]

1. Italo Calvino: *Six Memos for the Next Millennium*, Jonathan Cape, 1992.
2. Benjamin Buchloh: *Gabriel Orozco*, Kunsthalle Zurich, ICA London, DAAD Berlin, 1996.
3. Roland Barthes: 'Mythologies', *The New Citroen*, Paladin Books, 1973 (translated by Annette Larry). First published 1957.
4. See: Jean Fisher, 'The Sleep of Wakefulness', *Gabriel Orozco*, Kanaal Art Foundation,1993.
5. 'Gabriel Orozco' - Triunfo de la libertad No 18, Tlalpan, C.P. 1400. Editor Hans-Ulrich Obrist. Oktagon Verlag, Stuttgart,1995.
6. Italo Calvino, ibid.

The Framer's Collection
Testaments Preserved

JOHN GOTO

THE GREAT PATRONS of fine art today are not Charles Saatchi, the Arts Council or the Tate Gallery but the artists themselves, who finance the enterprise to an extent they do not recognise, and are impoverished in the process. Part of my meagre income comes from frame-making, using skills learnt from my grandfather, who was also a maker of coffins. My collection reflects upon the history of our century, and I feel an obligation to preserve those traces ignored by orthodox histories. The time has passed when narrative artists could assume a common store of myths with their audience. It falls to me therefore to tell what I know of these images; the rest has yet to be invented.

1. *Djadyad* by John Goto

Of my fondly remembered youth, few photographs and even fewer friends remain. These scraps survive from a journey to the disputed border territory where is situated the walled oasis town of Djadyad, then under the sway of Gram Moncur and his mercenaries. Linden, my travelling companion, was a spiritual young man with the appearance of a bandit from a Glauber Rocha movie. 'All things are interrelated,' he would tell me, 'our task is simply to find the true links.' We parted company at Djadyad, while he crossed the border in search of a Bedouin shaman reputed to be naming the grains of the desert sands; I returned to Europe.

2. *The Club* by Dorcus Walker

As a documentary photographer of the old school, Dorcus Walker believes in the veracity of the image and its social worth. Increasingly, however, such ideas seem outmoded as does her insistence on class as an instrument of social analysis. This particular image was taken outside an exclusive London club hosting the annual dinner of the ancient Mackerel Union.

3. *Portrait of Nadyezhda Vyetrova* (attributed to Nikolai Panov or Boris Molchanov, c. 1923)

Nadyezhda Vyetrova had married Nikolai Panov in 1917. However, at the time this painting was made, she was involved in an affair which she had been coerced into by the opportunistic Boris Molchanov. The view in the painting of St Savior Cathedral indicates that it was painted in Molchanov's studio. Panov, unaware of his wife's infidelity was then making a likeness of Molchanov, which also appears unfinished in Nadyezhda's portrait.

On discovering the affair, Panov left Moscow a broken man, and painted little before his death in the siege of Leningrad. Molchanov's career on the other hand advanced rapidly through the patronage of General Kliment Voroshilov and later the Kremlin, until by the thirties he had attained both power and influence. Nevertheless he did nothing to save Nadya when she was arrested on the orders of the Peoples' Commissar for Internal Affairs. Of the three, only Molchanov survived into the post-war period. An account of his career as a court painter may be read in any Soviet history.

4. *Untitled* by Salvatore Manzu

This photograph of a sentinel patrolling the E.U.R., Mussolini's civic project for Rome, is one of a number I own in a style, which, starting in Russia at the time of revolution, spread across Europe like an ink stain on a map, regardless of frontier or ideology. It was for a brief moment as if the socialists, capitalists, fascists and liberals collaborated on a collective dream named 'Futura'.

5. *An English Lady* by Bruno Essen

Recently I attended a conference in Oxford entitled 'Stalin Reassessed' and over lunch made the acquaintance of an elderly woman who had travelled widely in Europe between the wars. When she heard of my interests, she invited me to her apartment to view her collection. Although it contained much that was characteristic of the era, it was this particular painting that held my attention. At first she was reluctant to speak of it, but eventually relented and told of its genesis.

From a wealthy family, her sister also had a taste for travel and adventure, but the family became worried when, in Germany, she fell under the spell of the Nazi party. As a placatory gift to her parents she commissioned Bruno Essen to make this study of her by her beloved Tauber river. When war broke out, unable to live with her conflicting loyalties, she returned to this spot and shot herself in the head. My acquaintance kindly allowed me to copy the painting on condition that her identity and that of her sister remain anonymous.

6. *The Inheritance*

This still from the 1924 film, *The Inheritance*, is surely one of the defining moments of British Cinema. In it we see the young socialist, Archie Craig, gaining carnal knowledge of Lord Bentwhistle's youngest daughter, Isodora. The two are discovered by the hounds, and a hilarious scene ensues, as Craig is set upon by the dogs and their aristocratic masters.

My friend Dorcus Walker claims that we are witnessing the conception of New Labour, but I think that this is just one of her jokes.

7. *11th February 1949*

This photograph by my father, is of my mother on the day that I was born, and I am naturally very fond of it. When the contractions temporarily abated, my mother, who has always been a keen film buff, discharged herself from the Middlesex Hospital in time to catch the 1.39 pm performance of *Paisa* at the Academy Cinema. The film had received mixed reviews; the critics felt its formal beauty was marred by its anti-British sentiments, particularly the scene in which two British officers discuss architectural history whilst partisans die within their view. Mum loved it and my birth occurred without too much distress later that evening. I have always thought she looks a little like Ingrid Bergman in this photograph.

8. *The Death of a Child*

I bought this image in Helsinki. The Finns still have a convention of making photographs at funerals and this is obviously a fake, reminiscent of those made by James Van Der Zee in Harlem, as solace for grieving customers.

9. *L'Inconnue de la Seine*

The discovery of the body of a young woman in the Seine was in itself unremarkable, and yet her identity and the circumstances surrounding her death haunted the popular imagination for nearly a century, until this photograph came to light in Latin America. Moved by her beauty and serenity, an attendant at the city had taken a death mask from her face and later, mass-produced, it became a curio to be seen in houses across France.

It was whilst in Buenos Aires, attending a conference dedicated to Jorge Luis Borges on *The Myth of the Gaucho*, that Dr Harry Battley found this carte-de-visite in a junk shop. The face seemed familiar and on returning to London he referred to his copy of *Das ewige Antlitz* and confirmed that this was indeed the young woman found in the Seine. His curiosity roused, Battley determined to solve the mystery. Two clues within the picture proved vital to his enquiry - the brooch worn by the woman and a contaminating finger-print in the fabric of the photograph that had become more visible with time. Battley discovered that the setting was designed by Marcus Villard for a wealthy bon viveur, Monsieur Roland Vittes. A visit to Vittes' elderly daughter allowed him access to her parents papers, amongst which he found a note, from husband to wife, vehemently denying acquaintance with 'the Hungarian woman Ewa Lazlo'. Further enquiries confirmed that a music-hall artist of that name, whose description fitted the photograph, had performed at the Théâtre de Funambules during the summer in question. Although the identity of L'Inconnue seemed now to be established, the circumstances of her death were not.

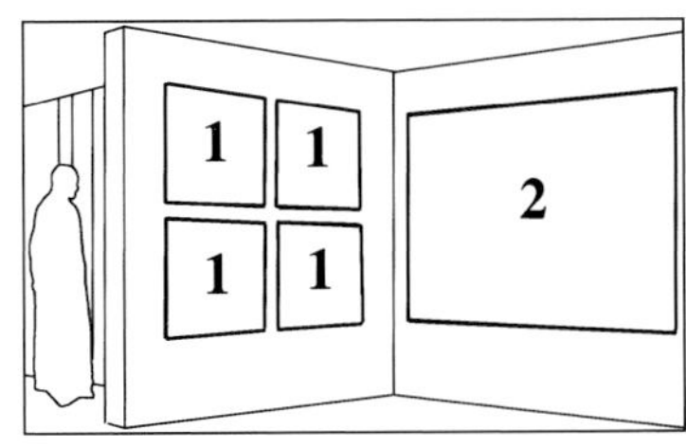

INSTALLATION VIEW I

Battley began his investigations into the finger-print at the records office of the Préfecture de Police in Paris but was disappointed to learn that they had not started taking prints until 1913. An unexpected piece of good fortune awaited him in Argentina; records went back to 1894 and the print was matched to that of a convicted blackmailer, Louis Argon. It was Argon's bad luck that, fleeing France, he should pick Buenos Aires where the Croatian immigrant Juan Vucetich was already operating his comparative finger-printing system within the police department. Dr Battley asserts that Argon fled the country after a failed attempt to blackmail Vittes about his liaison with the actress. The long held belief that L'Inconnue committed suicide now appears less likely than that she met her end at the hands of Louis Argon. The records in Buenos Aires also reveal that Argon was murdered in the last year of the century, knifed in a bar-room brawl by a gaucho.

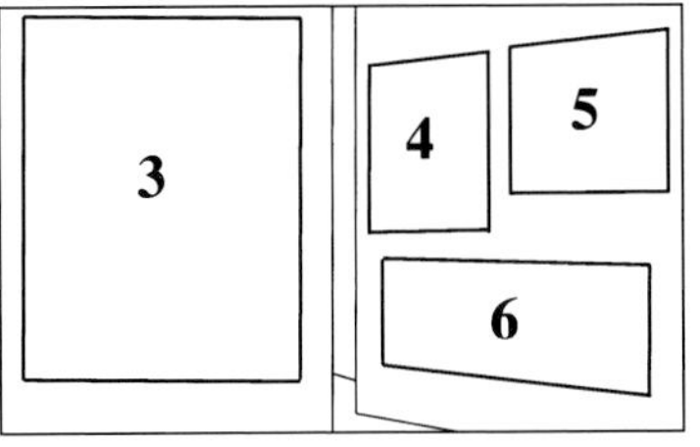

INSTALLATION VIEW II

10. *St James's, Piccadilly*

I have allowed myself one small indulgence in the collection and included this family snapshot, taken by my mother of my niece, on a day trip to London in 1983. It is of no historic interest, but I love the sense of trust and tenderness between the two women.... a moment of grace.

INSTALLATION VIEW III

11. *The Children*

Whilst studying in Paris in the late 1970s, I had an affair with an older woman. At times when I needed to escape its intensity, I would walk to the flea market at Porte de Clignancourt, which is where I found this photograph. What I particularly like about it is the poor cropping which allows us to see beyond the backdrop to the woman. It offers a cautionary tale to artists, warning that reality has an unruly habit of disrupting our symmetrical phantasies, and, as if further proof were required, this text is completed on my hospital bed, from where neither art nor the past can rescue me.

Multiple Darkness
Susan Trangmar

CHRISTOPHER WANT

IN A TEXT accompanying the publication of a selection of images from the series *Untitled Landscapes*, Susan Trangmar wrote affirmatively of 'the awful pleasure of multiplicity'[1]. Whilst this statement was written some ten years ago, it provides the leitmotif to the artist's continuing interests and concerns. For Trangmar, multiplicity and desire seem to be regarded in a way which suggests that what might be viewed as painful or uncomfortable is understood to be integral to pleasure. Trangmar's work engages with the 'space' of such intensity by incorporating, and even exploiting, potentially nihilistic tendencies as they emerge from the individual or collective subject's psyche, rather than from 'outside'.

Entry to the darkened exhibition space of **Exposures**[2] is via a short corridor constructed to keep out natural light. Some adjustment is needed once beyond the threshold. But this is not simply, or only, a matter of 'getting used' to the space, as the problem, or rather question, of adjustment and change remains inherent to the viewing and experience of the installation. This is why it would be too melodramatic to suggest that the visitor experiences a sense of disorientation within the gallery or detachment from its space. Rather, there is an idea of a transition, whereby the subject undergoes a movement from one interior space to other interiors. Trangmar introduces a series of thresholds between different interiors: the installation space, underground space, and the viewer's own internal space. Darkness predominates, but in the hidden form of different darknesses.

The installation consists of five projectors, unobtrusively suspended from the ceiling beyond the immediate proximity of the viewer. Facing different walls of the gallery, two of these projectors emit a single image of an empty mine tunnel. Set on a pulse, the images dissolve at intermittent intervals. The remaining projectors display carousels of images of the mines and the mine workers; these are set on a programme, the images dissolving at different rates. As a way of finding a purpose to the programming of the images, the viewer may try to detect an order to the sequentiality of the dissolves, either by focusing upon the timing of the issue of images from one of the projectors or, more difficult, by comparing several of the projectors' timings together. But this task seems impossible to fulfil since the timing turns out to be random, yet we continue to search for order. The succeeding experience is not quite one of 'sitting back and enjoying the show', for the confusion of the images' timing persists in their showing. But it turns out that this has the effect of maintaining an awareness of the surrounding display of images, even whilst trying to engage with one of the projections. There is, therefore, a persistent sense of distraction in connection to the experience of the installation as the viewer attempts variously to compare, differentiate and unify several or more of its components.

This is countered by an uncanny sense of absorption. The viewer is drawn into the space of the installation, to look at the images, to discern their relationship and gauge the effect of the timings and dissolves. But the installation does not cohere either at the level of narrative or at the level of a controlling authorial presence.

The recurrent images of tunnels viewed in perspective implies an exteriorising movement towards an (unknown) object in order to see and witness the 'outside'. Such a narrative would imply that we might escape our own finite limits and recognise ourselves in our desires and fears of the unknown. Trangmar's photographs of tunnels reiterate this impossible desire to see, and escape, desire. Their unceasing repetitiveness seems to assure a pleasure of recognition; even as the image dissolves it seems to beckon towards the viewer and draw upon a secret complicity.

Between the uncontrollable impulse to surpass our limits and the need to recognise ourselves in this obsession, there seems only to lie a debilitating sense of ending and finality. These images of empty mine shafts seem to trace this very sense of redundancy. Pallid and green in the luminescence, they absorb the potential for material form. Even their emptiness will soon disappear as they are sealed up and abandoned to the entropic processes of subterranean earth.

On three further projectors other images are juxtaposed with the mine tunnels. Taken at the cliff face, in proximity to the machines and the miners, these photographs are all hand-held and shot on long exposures. Against the dark of the mines, traces of light are left by the miners lamps and the illuminations on the coal face machinery and the transport wagons. In Trangmar's transformation, flickers smear and line the surface of the images; light bursts in brilliant cascades; fire seems to burn in the darkness, a raw energy blinding in itself but offering a brief interruptive sight of an elemental and ravaged terrain. The dark is enveloping, but here and there confused glimpses are caught of the propped-up mine shaft ceilings and of the movements of the miners at work. Atop machinery, or in transit, the figures of the miners are blurred and streaked, although some details remain in the flare: a face turned towards the camera, a miner in a vest at the controls of an excavator, a tattooed arm resting on the frame of a wagon. In other images, miners - it's hard to tell how many - walk towards the camera, already overtaken by the glare of their lamps etched in the film.

Owing to the low lighting in the mines and the limitations of the technical medium the subject is prevented from seeing and recognising what is before her. As a consequence, images are invariably composed across the picture plane. The streaks of light often still seem to describe a perspectival movement towards an object but, in fact, they demarcate a movement across the camera lens and away from it.

The different emissions of light traced upon the slides parallel the projections across the gallery wall. Despite the journey through the mines, or our progress through the gallery space, neither tells a story or takes us anywhere; they form a random and scattered collection of affects which indicate the subject's desire either to anticipate and seek out the object, or defend herself against its threat.

Regardless of the technical limitations imposed upon the artist by the subterranean environment and her attempts to relinquish control of the outcome of the photographic process, there still results a recurrence of the impossible and nihilistic desire to witness the object. Trangmar's installation provides evidence of the endless dialectic between constructive and destructive tendencies attendant upon the desire to recognise and witness ourselves. Her project is formed by such a desire and inevitably it operates within its limits. But the artist's interest in multiplicity is such that the affirmatory experience of desire is necessarily bound to painful feelings of guilt and shame, even whilst it revalues them.

What is at stake is a revaluation of the relationship between a sense of force and the instinct for pleasure. These two phenomena are vital components of the artistic and creative process, but they can only coexist, or work together, by virtue of a process of severance. This was signalled in some of Trangmar's earliest works, such as the series *Untitled Landscapes*, by the shadowy presence of the artist in the foreground of the images with her back turned away from the viewer.

By means of this stark but unconditional refusal the artist detaches herself, even rejects, the outside viewer. Inevitably, this results in troubling feelings of frustration and alienation by anyone wishing to engage with the images. But, at the same time, the viewer is placed in a fortunate position: some of the onus of responsibility which the subject feels towards the image - not only to understand and decipher it, but also to maintain its possibility as a site of meaning - is removed by the insertion of the artist's presence into these 'landscapes'. However, the image does not belong to the artist, even though she reaffirms her attachment to it in severing herself from the viewer's gaze. Instead the process of severance enables both artist and viewer, both of whom are positioned before the image, to witness (again) its primordiality as illusion. The 'landscape' as object of the gaze exists despite the subject. The scene in front of them cannot be eliminated, although the subject may disappear from the scene. In many of the landscape images the subject appears as a silhouette lost in their own darkness.

UNTITLED LANDSCAPES (DETAIL), 1985

Such 'witnessing' in Trangmar's work is oriented towards, and produced by, *darkness* - which is nothing other than the force allowing the image to be formed as a lack. And, it is by virtue of darkness - the 'dark' artist/viewer positioned before the images - that the illusion and the 'presence' of our fascinated gaze, is maintained. Watching the caged rhinoceroses, in an image from *Untitled Landscapes*, the subject is riveted by, and excluded from, the scene, which repeats the dynamics of the fantasy of the primal scene. Part of these dynamics would involve a fear of the subject's disappearance before nature. In Trangmar's work the figure of the artist/viewer remains, but hidden in darkness.

EXPOSURES (DETAIL), 1996

Darkness is used in the **Exposures** installation precisely not to expose the object of desire (i.e. the subject), but to hide and cloak a multiplicity: a dispersed subject which would disintegrate in the light of exposure. This is where Trangmar's sense of affirmation is situated, at the very point where a boundless sense of nihilism is brought into form, albeit a dark one, and, therefore, reveals itself not as void, but as *transformation*.

1. Susan Trangmar, *Untitled Landscapes*, *Ten 8*, no. 25, 1987, p. 29.
2. *Exposures*, Angel Row Gallery, Nottingham, 21 May - 22 June, 1996.

Thwarted Vision

New Works by Willie Doherty

DAVID GREEN

ONE OF THE large projected images in Willie Doherty's installation *The Only Good One is a Dead One* is a view, seen from the interior of a stationary car, of a street in an urban housing estate at night. On the opposite wall and in the opposite corner of the gallery space, a second image is projected. The scene, once again, is shot through the windscreen of a car at night, but the car is now moving along narrow country roads, from which the lights of a city can occasionally be seen in the distance. Although held together in terms of relationships of both their formal similarities and differences, the two images are physically and perceptually dislocated from each other by a spatial arrangement which precludes the possibility of the viewer seeing both simultaneously. Situated between the two, the viewer is forced to turn and move from one image to the other, to view each alternatively, negotiating the darkened space that is barely illuminated by the reflected light from the image screens. The sense of disorientation that this involves is further compounded by the accompanying soundtrack. This consists of an anonymous male voice, at times despondent at others excited, that delivers what might be construed as an interior monologue, a kind of stream of unconscious thought that we are unexpectedly privy to. Equally, however, it might be that what we are listening to is part of a conversation into which we are implicitly drawn as correspondents, albeit temporarily silent. Either way, as the account we hear oscillates between the speaker's fears of being a victim and imaging his own death to the fantasy of his being an assassin, we seem engaged as unwilling agents in these melodramatic scenarios of violence and revenge. There is no reason to associate the disjointed narrative which this voice offers us with the projected image sequences but inevitably, it would seem, we assume that the voice belongs to someone who occupies the car, and with him we sit and watch, or sit and drive, compelled to adopt his point of view (the point of view the camera gives us) just as we are compelled to be his confidant.

The ways in which the spectator is physically and psychically positioned by the operations and structures of vision and language, or image and text, has often been acknowledged as a key feature of Doherty's work. In the case of the visual image, for example, the notion of 'point of view' involves the viewer not only in terms of a physical relationship to the image but it also indicates a point at which he or she is psychologically bound into the image and, therefore, reflexively positioned by it. It could be said that the point of view of the image calls the viewer into being, positioning him or her in a place in which their identity as a viewing subject is precisely articulated. In a similar fashion, language operates to produce a reader (or listener) not only of, but also for, the text. This strategic implication of the viewer/reader in the subject positions and identities that may be seen as prescribed within vision and language, takes on, however, particular resonance in the historical, political and geographic context in which Doherty's practice has almost invariably been situated. Jean Fisher, for example, has perceptively drawn a direct parallel between Doherty's manipulation and positioning of the viewer/reader in terms of 'the duplicity of identity and difference' and 'a psychosis that haunts the imaginary relation between self and Other in colonialist discourse'.[1] The colonialist discourse in question here is that which continues to plague the historical relationship between Britain and Ireland and which continues to provide the dynamic of political division and sectarian conflict and violence in the North. In this context the politics of identity and difference is never an idle theoretical affair; it assumes a gruesome reality on a regular day-to-day basis.

Doherty's work has consistently explored the mechanisms of vision and language to reveal the structures of alterity embedded therein, and nowhere more so than in relationship to the power of the gaze. The gaze is the recurrent motif in much of Doherty's early work; it's omnipotence, vigilance and mastery clearly aligned to a society in which surveillance is the prerequisite of control. Thus many of Doherty's images have invoked the kind of precise organisation of reality for the camera which presumes a distanced vantage point outside the flux of events, a transcendent point of vision, a point at which the scene is gathered together, ordered and fixed. Of course, the logic of such a system of visual representation opens out the possibility of its direct inversion. The point of view of the gaze is a place from which the viewer 'fixes' the scene before her but it is also the point at which she herself is fixed, and the potential for the simple reversal of the axis of vision would mean that the gaze is always capable of being returned. Thus Doherty has also produced images in which the place occupied by the viewer - the camera's point of view - takes on aspects of openness and vulnerability, and with this the viewer is positioned as the potential object rather than the subject of an (unseen) controlling gaze.

The gaze, however, can only operate in the realm of absolute visibility. That is to say, it demands a set of conditions in which the field of vision is uninterrupted and the object of sight fully exposed. Yet this is precisely what much of Doherty's more recent work denies us. What interests me about the projected video images in the *The Only Good One is a Dead One* is precisely their frustration of any attempt to see clearly what is represented. The static view framed from within the interior of the car might ostensibly offer some kind of voyeuristic pleasure but the artificial haze of street lights, further refracted and distorted within the windscreen, denies the viewer any easy access to what might be happening. And whilst in the glare of the headlamps of the moving car the scene before us is brightly lit, it vanishes almost as soon as it appears, existing barely as a fleeting memory. I think it is not coincidental, therefore, that many of Doherty's more recent photographic works similarly involve a resistance to the gaze, and the use of various devices by which vision is, partially at least, thwarted. The most obvious of these devices is simply the absence of that which makes vision possible. In images such as *Unapproved Road* and *Alleyway*, both of 1992, light barely penetrates the space before the camera, leaving what is perceptible to the eye as only partial evidence and what lies beyond condemned to the realm of the unknown.

In other ways too, the camera's gaze and with it what we might take to be the natural propensity of the photographic image, has been literally deflected, baffled and obscured. In *Bullet Holes* (1995) the compression of the camera's depth of field leaves relatively little of the image in focus, and both this image and *Minor Incident 2* (1994) are characteristic of a marked trend in Doherty's work which consists of closing down the field of vision and filling the frame with some detail or fragment of an object or scene. And whilst he has not entirely abandoned the devices of the gaze as it penetrates deep into the space before it, Doherty seems increasingly drawn in some of his images to exclude any suggestion of dramatic spatial recession and therefore, to a greater or lesser extent, to emphasise the literal flatness of image. In the most recent series of photoworks entitled *Disclosures*, three dimensional space gives way to the conscious and deliberate manipulation of the two dimensional co-ordinates of the surface, and the exaggerated articulation of the image *as* image.[2] Thus, by means of its internal lateral bisection, its arrangement of shapes (mostly) parallel to the picture plane, and its mapping of pregiven grids, these images attest to a geometricisation and ordering of the surface of the image over and above whatever that image might depict. No longer orientated exclusively to the order of an external referent, these photographs are more closely aligned to the modernist 'surface', and apparently subject to its laws of pure aesthetic integrity. In *Factory (Reconstruction)* (1995), too, one finds a similar flattening of vision; the scattered debris that litters the floor and peeling paintwork of the walls conjoin with the picture plane and a scene of disorder and chaos is transformed into an aesthetically seductive surface.

Increasingly it would seem that the rigid Euclidian geometry of space in Doherty's work of the 1980s has given way to an insistence upon the opacity of the two dimensional surface, and, relatedly, the specificities of place, which featured so strongly in terms of the political geography of Northern Ireland, have been replaced by an iconography that is effectively siteless. Or so it would appear. That this work involves what might be termed the aestheticisation of reality there can be little doubt, and many of his images owe much to the sensibilities of a highly schooled modernist eye. Yet, however much photography is able to gain a certain distance from its referential function when it is framed by the discourse of the aesthetic, the indexical power of the photograph can never entirely be suspended and the trace of the 'real' will always reassert itself. Doherty's photographic practice trades on this kind of ambivalence, always hovering somewhere between the modernist aesthetic and the documentary record, but the purpose for doing so is clearly strategic. In the end, of course, Doherty's recent work resists any facile reading in terms of its purely formal and aesthetic qualities; any rudimentary knowledge of the historical and political context of his practice would certainly preclude this. On the other hand, whilst these images appear to attest to that inevitable seepage of the index that has cast photography in its role as an infallible witness, they also theatricalise the real, leaving us unsure as to where the boundaries between fact and fiction may lie. Like the liminal spaces that are so often the subject of his photographs, Doherty's work occupies a territory without clearly demarcated borders. Finding a way through is the first task for the viewer.

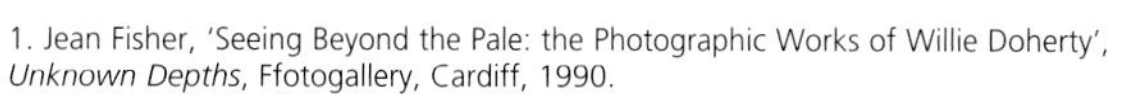

1. Jean Fisher, 'Seeing Beyond the Pale: the Photographic Works of Willie Doherty', *Unknown Depths*, Ffotogallery, Cardiff, 1990.

2. The series of three photoworks entitled *Disclosures* were produced for an exhibition featuring the work of Willie Doherty, Terry Atkinson and John Goto that I co-curated for the University of Brighton Gallery in November 1996. I discuss these works in more detail in my catalogue essay 'Refiguring Identity, Retouching History, Revisioning Art', in *Circumstantial Evidence*, University of Brighton, 1996.

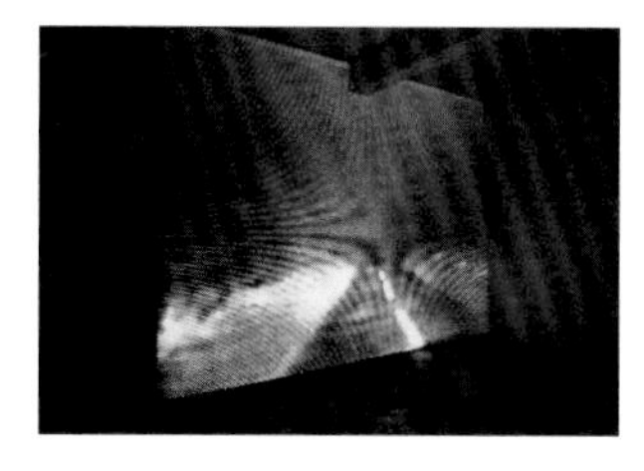

THE ONLY GOOD ONE IS A DEAD ONE, 1993

AT THE BORDER 1 (WALKING TOWARDS A MILITARY CHECKPOINT), 1995

UNAPPROVED ROAD 2, 1995

Family Photographs
Richard Billingham

MARK DURDEN

RICHARD BILLINGHAM'S PICTURES are uncaptioned, raw colour images sequenced in book form[1] or displayed in art galleries[2]. They relate to both documentary and snapshot photography. They involve the appeal to emotion that is at the heart of the documentary genre, images of poverty which call upon the tradition of photography involved in the transgressive and guilt-ridden act of looking across classes, of seeing how 'the other half lives'[3]. As documentary photos they elide private and public spheres, are responsible for what Roland Barthes has referred to as photography's 'explosion of the private into the public, or rather into the creation of a new social value, which is the publicity of the private...'[4]

Billingham has told us something of the background to these pictures. They are photos of his close family: his unemployed alcoholic father, Ray; his mother Elizabeth who hardly drinks but smokes a lot and likes pets and things that are decorative; his brother Jason who was taken into care when eleven, but is now back with Ray and Liz again[5]. All are pictured in their small and crammed Birmingham flat. Of his family's response to the book, Billingham has said how: 'Neither I nor they are shocked by its directness because we're all well-enough acquainted with having to live with poverty. After all, there are millions of other people in Britain living similarly... It is certainly not my intention to shock, to offend, sensationalise, be political or whatever. Only to make work that is as spiritually meaningful as I can make it. Whatever the medium.'[6]

As family photographs they have the qualities of snapshots, the seeming artlessness of the amateur photo. Billingham even had them processed at the local chemists, and many evidently came back with 'quality control' stickers on them. Ordinarily the imagery of snapshots secures a longed-for cohesion of the family group. In his sociological study of amateur photographs, Pierre Bourdieu pointed out their particular role. They are involved in 'solemnizing and immortalizing the high points of family life, in short, of reinforcing the integration of the family group by reasserting the sense that it has both of itself and of its unity.'[7] The photo album full of 'good moments' and 'good memories' reassures us of the family's solidity and cohesion. Yet while both the context and character of amateur photography inform Richard Billingham's work, what we witness is an uncompromising focus on the dark side of family life - the violence and trauma of alcoholism and abject poverty.

There's something decidedly incongruous about the colour snapshot being blown up and displayed as a collectible art photograph in the gallery. Yet for all the flaws and imperfections, the visual effect, the style of these pictures, is deliberate and knowing. His pictures possess a distinctive visual richness, an understanding of form - Billingham's photos of his family were initially taken as reference material for paintings while an art student at Sunderland University. Their formal awareness in large part stems from an excess of detail, of decoration, a kitsch ornamentation which seems somewhat in contradistinction to the often unpleasant traumas of the family life depicted. Billingham often accents formal correspondences, makes a series of visual puns in his pictures. One of Billingham's most visually rich is a portrait of his mother doing a jigsaw puzzle which sets up collisions between its mosaic of colours, the blue box of 'Sky' cigarettes on the half-formed jigsaw landscape on the table top, the box of jigsaw pieces and his mother's floral dress. In the picture showing a potentially violent argument with Ray Billingham's wife looking as though she's about to thump her husband - and with Richard Billingham's brother hovering awkwardly in the background and only just intruding into frame - what is also caught is a visual interplay of patterns, the floral tattoos all over Mrs Billingham's arm, the pattern on her dress, the wallpaper and all those ornaments on the cabinet shelves in the background. This visual richness contradicts and forestalls the realist punch of the picture.

Aesthetics has always been a problem with documentary. Walker Evans found beauty in the interiors and meagre possessions of the three tenant farmer families he photographed at the time of the American Depression. While these pictures were published uncaptioned, James Agee worried over the privilege of an educated sight in the 471 text which accompanied them. 'To those who own and create it' the beauty of the sharecroppers' homes was 'irrelevant and indiscernible.'[8] It was only seen by 'those who by economic advantages of training have only a shameful and thief's right to it: and it might be said that they have any "rights" whatever only in proportion as they recognise the ugliness and disgrace implicit in their privilege of perception.'[9] Agee even went so far as to say that 'the "sense of beauty", like nearly everything else, is a class privilege.'[10]

The documentary by Evans and Agee is marked by class difference and guilt about that difference. The photographer and writer remained spies, outsiders, speaking for and representing those denied a means of self-representation. Billingham's is not in this sense a document of another social group, but his own family. His pictures are to an extent autobiographic. Nick Waplington's documentary practice comes closest to Billingham's photography. But even here, important differences remain. Billingham is much closer to those he represents than Waplington. Waplington can only assume a close relationship, put himself literally in the picture of his close friends, the two Nottingham families living on a council estate he photographed for the *Living Room* series. As Irvine Welsh puts it: 'You see Nick appearing as much as subject as anyone else engaging in the joke, mucking about.'[11] In the positive reception of this work, 'intimacy' and 'generosity' are qualities referred to as a means of offsetting the accusations of voyeurism and intrusion his work has encountered. Waplington's use of a medium-format camera gives his images the opposite effect of Billingham's snapshots - a grandeur and space to those depicted and an art historical import. John Berger sees them as 'next-door neighbours to those of baroque ceiling painting and, in particular to the work of Peter Paul Rubens. There is an extraordinary affinity of colour, pose, gesture, framing, composition...'[12] They are involved with the visual dynamic of the baroque, in which the earth-bound is moved into the celestial. They go beyond, or as Welsh puts it, 'transcend by miles mere social documentary.'[13]

There's a certain instability to some of Billingham's pictures - an effect particular to snapshot photography, a love of the frozen moment, the expressive instant: the comic and bizarre picture in which Ray Billingham looks as though he has just thrown one of the cats in the air, and another in which he is caught falling towards the frame of a picture on the carpet. The instabilities of this family life are matched by the qualities of some of its pictures. There's a sense of disorder, social disturbance and violence: from peas and carrots spilt on the kitchen floor to pictures showing both Ray Billingham and his wife with blood on their faces or him slumped by a stained toilet. Both the grainy and hazy portrait of Ray Billingham taken in low light and the blurred portrait of him on the cover of the book, seem intended to mirror his semi-conscious, drunken state. Yet despite such an evident expressive use of photography, we cannot fully know these people, for all the evident intimacy of their depiction, they will always remain apart, aloof. These pictures can offer only fragments of this dramatic life, much invariably remains unexplained and unknown.

Realism is always at odds with the aesthetic. Hegel's 'Lectures On Aesthetics' set an ideal of beauty against realist art. He condemned portrait painters who were content merely to imitate their models without improving upon them, without raising them up to the ideal[14]. In the early discourses around photography, it was details which were seen to prevent photography from rivalling the style of the work of art. Portrait photography's detailism meant the inauguration of new techniques of idealisation, of retouching photographs. With Billingham's extraordinary series of family pictures, it's the details which both concretise the uncomfortable reality of this family life, and also provide us with those decorative visual puns, the optical plenitude of certain images: the interplay between Liz Billingham's dress and the tiny jigsaw pieces, for example. The allure of such visual effects rubs against the grain of photographic referentiality: the traumatic life depicted. If these photos attest to the close family group in which the son takes pictures of his parents and brother, he is at the same time a son trained at art school, one who brings certain aesthetic distinctions with him. While his photos might ape the informality and anti-aesthetic of the snapshot, a playful formalism persists. Our viewing of these pictures of working class family life is filtered through a certain aesthetic. The visual patterns and richness of these pictures keep pulling us away from the uneasy confrontation with the real. Richard Billingham's pictures set up an essentially conflicting relationship with the viewer. Ultimately, our formal and aesthetic interest in these prints confirms the irrevocable distance from the social reality depicted: these scenes of pain, violence and love.

RAY'S A LAUGH

RAY'S A LAUGH

RAY'S A LAUGH

1. Richard Billingham, *Ray's A Laugh*, Zurich, Berlin and New York, Scalo Press, 1996.
2. I first saw Richard Billingham's photographs in a group show at Anthony Reynolds, London, in 1995. This essay is written in response to the work exhibited at the National Museum of Photography, Film and Television, Bradford, 14 September to 17 November, 1996.
3. For a recent detailed discussion of the politics of documentary in print, photography and film see Paula Rabinowitz's *They Must Be Represented*, London, Verso, 1990.
4. Roland Barthes, *Camera Lucida*, London, Cape, 1981, p. 98.
5. I should add something here about the use of first names. The title of the book *Ray's a Laugh* and the short description by Billingham about the members of his family on its backcover, encourages the viewer to also refer to them by their first names, a familiarity which tends to disguise the true distance which exists between ourselves and these people.
6. Statement accompanying a series of photographs in *Camera Austria International*, August 1996, p. 4.
7. Pierre Bourdieu, *Photography, A Middle-brow Art*, Cambridge, Polity Press, 1996, p. 19.
8. James Agee, *Let Us Now Praise Famous Men*, London: Peter Owen, 1975, p. 203.
9. Ibid., p. 203.
10. Ibid., p. 314.
11. Irvine Welsh, 'Postscript' to Nick Waplington, *Weddings, Parties, Anything*, New York, Aperture, 1996, n.p.
12. John Berger, 'Means to Live' in Nick Waplington, *Living Room*, Manchester, Cornerhouse Publications, 1991, n.p.
13. Welsh, op.cit. n.p.
14. For a brilliant discussion of Hegel's *Aesthetics* see Naomi Schor's *Reading in Detail*, London: Methuen, 1987, pp. 23-41.

Maps of Melancholy

Jim Mooney

STELLA SANTACATTERINA

THE WORK OF Jim Mooney distances itself from the currency of postmodernism. He is not concerned with the interminable referentiality of current practice; rather, art for him must create or form a dialogue with existence or the being of man. His work refers to the traditions of painting in different ways, such as, for example, Italian fresco. The external archetype of his work is reminiscent of the form of Paolo Uccello's paintings; he establishes a mutually interrogative relationship between the history of painting and the practice of photography. The interweaving of form and image create an erotic movement which concerns the body and the space which surrounds it. Space and time become suffocated and compressed psychic substance, material presence. The continuous oscillation of desire creates movement through the pressure of surface and depth, visibility and invisibility; desire does not only articulate a movement backwards and forwards, but also in and out. This rhythmic quality gives to the image the appearance of bi-dimensionality similar to the bas-relief; a proportional relationship between the microcosm of language and the macrocosm of reality is created.

The artist deals with the internal mechanism of painting in the construction of the pictorial image: the marks, the stains, which constitute the photograph, initiate a recognition of absence which they themselves articulate as a vertiginous space. Just as the footprint is a silent witness to the past presence of a human being, so the stains are indexical traces of the unspeakable and unrepresentable, what, in Lacanian terms we might call the dark knot of language. As Henry Rogers writes of this work, 'in the spatio-temporal experience the image, object, body and text are interwoven through desire, mourning and loss.' But at the same time, the artist's work is surrounded by an atmosphere of cold, where the body is frozen in its own impression, deprived of its own subjectivity: this means in effect, it is without psychology. Finally, it is left in a state of impersonality, where phenomenological appearance comes into existence. The body as the language of art is not the field of extension or the breakdown of limits, but a dialectic place where we measure the relationship between subject and object. This is emphasised in various works where the photographic substrate reiterates the function of the veil and operates as a porous surface or semi-permeable membrane which allows for the establishment of an osmotic relationship between the interiority of the unconscious and the conscious extroversion of language as artistic practice. Through this relationship it becomes possible to create an image of the self in which narcissism reverses the position from the love of himself and inaugurates a relationship with the external.

Moreover, art is always a response to lack and inaugurates a process of loss or mourning. The language of art is always the continuous practice of desire born of absence and of the impossible. The naked body in Mooney's work functions as representation of an ambivalent Eros which registers at the same time the pleasure of possession and the contemporaneous pain of loss. This pain of loss becomes effective from the moment it is transferred to the zone of representation. Eroticism therefore is always a loss of the quotidian and becomes rather a desiring practice of absence and of impossibility. Absence glows visible. Therefore art does not consent to life but with the philosophy of life.

When life is the place of alterity, art is the place where the imaginary tries to achieve the lost unity. If, as Blanchot suggests, writing suspends death, this means it suspends the instant through a condensation of space and time. Here the signs/stains are traces which do not evoke other meanings beyond this instant. They do not, therefore require disappearance but show themselves as evidence in their own compression, which is, at the same time, a moment of time and death. The magic activity of the artist is to recreate the instant into a temporal symbol without any explanation of meaning. The only meaning is the trace as an act of existence.

In the work *Scotoma* (1995) the field of the image is determined by the modular repetition of the fold, which together with the metaphysics of black and white, introduces a further element of mourning, of loss. But without drama, because, after all, mourning is a tonality of the work itself, a veil on the surface of the image on which the forms flow. The horizontality of space vies with the horizontality of language, the dissolution of time (death), from the death of language, understood as repetition, which affirms itself in the repetition of the movement of the fold; a form of paralysis, the frozen dimension of life, struggles with the dimension of thought which prevents despair. Repetition, in fact, is generated in the absence of desire, inside the pretext of language where the drive of desire no longer runs freely but can only gently follow the line of its own representation. The consciousness of loss becomes the style of the lost. The face comes into being as visual image without losing density or consistency. It is, in fact, Plato who tells us that vision is the most acute of all the perceptions which come through the body. The kind of operation set up in the repetition of these works allows the artist to find a rhythm without a return; printed on the surface of the photographic image, which bears the paradoxical sensuality of black and white. 'A picture is composed with that infallible proportion of shadow, of relief and omission, of remembrance and oblivion' (Proust).

A Baroque melancholy surrounds Mooney's work: it pervades the paintings and photographs as well as objects. Emblematic is the photographic *Shroud* series (1996). Here the artist tends to represent the *horror vacui* of art itself through forms which present themselves as shadows of life itself. The forms created are symbolically abstract, reproducing an interior, virtual movement. The melancholic state is the preparatory condition for creativity, for the artistic consciousness that operates in the field of the virtuality of language and not in the reality of things. If the visible constitutes the recognisable landscape external to humankind, the artist opposes to it a formal universe related to his own invisible interiority. Mooney reverses the invitation of Klee to make visible the invisible and give the latter autonomy and concreteness. The invisible is extracted from the precarious banal visible of the everyday, and this is restored as the unique condition of art, and also of the artist himself.

This dynamic process is underlined with greater emphasis in another image, *Delire* (1995). In this work the artist transports with fluidity and detachment the element which characterises the city of Venice - water: an element which is murky and heavily-laden with image and history. Water's peculiarity is transparency, which produces fluidity, ambivalence, ambiguity and vertigo. It is a vertigo born of a circular succession of vision without beginning or end, and it introduces us to the space governed by the circular course of time, where the shadow and the image fluctuate and reflect each other in such a way as to create a fragmentation of the architecture of time. At this point it seems clear - also taking account of the work's title 'Delire' - that the relationship Mooney has with language is based on the consideration that it is language itself that constitutes the total reality to be confronted - the starting point from which to make experimentation, of a possible laceration, capable of finding a new articulation. It seems that he almost makes his own independent version of Klossowski's statement 'Each experimental initiative requires a delirious interpretation, extremely lucid.' Art always requires an 'experimental initiative' to reach a form capable of transforming the impulse of the imagination into an objective result. The experimentation is not, of course, concerned simply with the field of technique, but rather with the continuity of a vision which doesn't hesitate. The impulse of the artist finds in language the field in which the gesture becomes the visible trace. From the moment the artist moves under the pressure of personal necessity, and does not operate within an already preconceived plan, he requires the strength of an 'experimental initiative', which *per se* is confined to a state of delirium. 'Delire' means, etymologically speaking, to go out of line, to go beyond a previous knowledge of language. Mooney is an artist who has all the consciousness of this condition, the knowledge of the excess necessary to found a personal image. In order to reach a resultant form, he arms himself with lucidity to gain control of the delirium without reducing the intensity through the control that pure reason seeks to impose. His work is a formal condensation, the presence of an absence.

DELIRE, 1995

A harmonic and solemn silence surrounds the composition of the triptych, *Face to Face* (1995), here the form tends towards totality. The veil places upon the face, confers to the image, a statuary aura, it becomes the cast of an indestructible form, which is in fact, a transition to the place of immortality, where the gesture is definitive, no further intervention is possible. I mean by this, it reaches a perfect correspondence between feeling and visual form. The work doesn't designate the condition of fragments which deviate separately from the totality. The double expression of mourning and melancholy which emanates from the the image is stabilised through a Nietzschean pathos of distance towards language, the only reality upon which the artist may construct his own image. This distance allows him the necessary detachment to give to artistic practice its own potential intensity. It takes away from the figure, the object, any reference to the thing itself. Like Alice in Wonderland, Mooney knows how indispensable it is to go beyond the threshold of the mirror before the realisation of the work. In all his work there is this going beyond the threshold - from the pure specular relationship with things. He takes and assumes an 'experimental initiative' which emancipates him constantly from any condition of pure melancholy or transgression, and makes him capable of founding an harmonic, iconographic universe between his imagination and a spatio-temporal 'delire'.

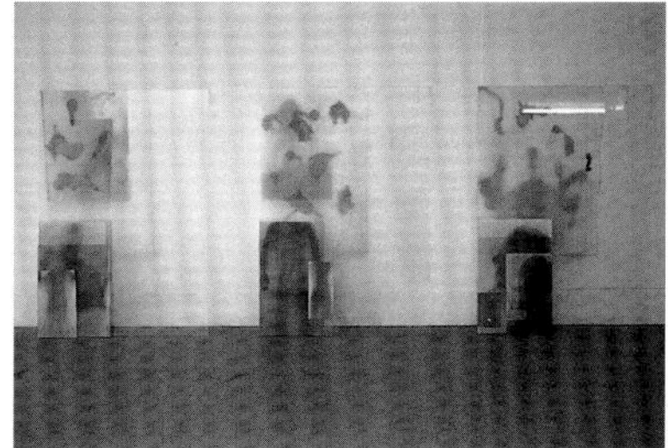

PROPOSITIONS I II & III, 1995

Cocks and Other Contradictions
The Works of Robert Mapplethorpe

SUNIL GUPTA

IN THIS ESSAY, I want to talk about the way in which Mapplethorpe's homo-erotic work positions a critique within a defence of the work, even if the critic is not particularly fond of the images and what they represent. I do not want to discuss the flowers and the portraits for the purposes of this essay. I want to discuss the way in which I became aware of the work and how the images have reappeared before me over the last twenty years, and how their meanings changed over time. I want to raise certain curiosities about the current show at the Hayward Gallery (London, October 1996). I want to discuss the parallel rise of gay political ideologies which coalesced into the various strategies to fight AIDS in North America and Europe. I want to discuss how all these issues relate to people of colour. Mapplethorpe's most notorious images are focused on black men and their sexuality/sexual organs. The period spanned, the mid-1970s to the mid-1990s, has another parallel; the acceptance of photography as art, particularly in the place where all the above issues were being fought over and where Mapplethorpe lived and worked - New York City. Americans claim to have invented modern photography and New York is where it found its most influential champions. Not too coincidentally, New York is also seen as the centre of the contemporary art world with the power to settle major issues such as this. Douglas Crimp has written about the cynical appropriation by the art world of photography in *The Ruins of the Museum*.

I am pointing out all these issues since at the cross-roads of all this arrived a lone practitioner, with an attitude towards photography that fitted right into modernism, just ripe for canonisation. I, too, arrived in New York at about the same time and very soon after my arrival got diverted from my studies into the photography world of workshops with Lisette Model, and hanging out with dealers who were buying Arbus pictures by the dozen for buyers in Houston during the day and spending their evenings at the Mineshaft. After a while, all this seemed terribly normal. To be trendy you had to be youngish, gay, male, built like a brick shit-house and hung like a horse. All kinds of sexual experimentation were both practised in public places and discussed in fashionable publications. *The Village Voice* sent a woman disguised as a leather man to check out the Mineshaft, and the inevitable experimentation led to the notion of the ultimate sexual trip - terminal sex.

It seemed inevitable that somebody would come and photograph it all. A fellow student of mine at the time, in a photo class, once declared that everything would be photographed - that peculiarly self-satisfied American notion that somehow technology would solve all our human relationship problems. Mapplethorpe appears to be seeking this position. He would photograph this underworld and make it explicit. Of course, there is an undeniable contradiction here, as the making explicit of something which at its core has desire intersecting with an illicit lust; a hidden expression of what we are capable of doing, if we dare, rather robs the activities of their personal satisfaction. It's rather like watching too many porno movies or spending too much time in a sauna - after a while there is no mythology left, nothing to hang your desire on, just the endlessly repeated nuts and bolts of the action. This is a feature of the Mapplethorpe photos that I find less interesting; at one level they are mechanical and shed a rather literal light on the human condition; they never seem to catch a moment of desire that might enigmatically engage our attention over a period of time. When it comes to 1970s New York gay scene photos, I much prefer the engaging scenarios of Arthur Tress.

Still, Mapplethorpe gives us *Man in Polyester Suit* - quite simply a big black dick hanging out of that quintessential American symbol of the working class - the polyester suit. Now, I bet there weren't any pictures of black penises on show in the art world before. I haven't got research on this, but we all know that the art world in America and Britain likes to retain its lily-white status. Feminists have asked where are the great women artists and blacks have asked where are the great black artists, but where indeed are the blacks even as subject matter? You might think I am exaggerating after 'Black Arts' appeared to sweep across the UK in the 1980s, but even today the visibility count is dreadfully low. It's another sad example of the failure of our equal opportunities policies.

The Mapplethorpe formula of race and gay sex was extremely opportunistic as it broke across two of the greatest taboos in society and appealed to a metropolitan audience who would be too sophisticated not to notice and dismiss the work as that of an upstart 'Drummer' photographer. What's intriguing me is how, on the face of it, such uninteresting photographs came to be canonised in the way that they have been. The style of placing the black men on pedestals and the appeal to racist America's fear of black sexuality has all been done before. Yet his pictures have appeared as a novelty. Any number of quite sensible people have rushed to their defence in the anti-censorship debates in America over the fracas engendered by the cancellation of his show at the

Corcoran in Washington.

It seems to me that they have become entangled in the politics of gay liberation. In the post-Stonewall 1970s atmosphere, the ideology of promiscuity became entrenched as a way of flaunting our difference. The occasional and very illegal toilet sexual encounter blossomed into the world of bath-houses and back-room bars. Once you've checked in your identity at the door along with your clothes, your body is free of any social constraints, and it seemed to be an ultimate coming together of politics and pleasure. Unlike some other liberation theologies of the time, this one offered you your cake and you could eat it too. Naturally, the body had to conform, but that was the largely ignored subtext. You can't shed your skin, so race, and consequently culture, became a barrier.[1]

For me, this binary opposition of black and white seemed to operate to the exclusion of all others. This is what is finally extremely irritating about the Mapplethorpe pictures; they follow the modernist position of showing what is, without referencing complexity. OK! so Robert liked black men, but in the work the racial issue is tantalisingly raised and then it doesn't go anywhere. Ultimately, it's symbolic of the reductive nature of 1970s gay semiotics. People fashioned specialised sexual roles and advertised them in direct uncomplicated ways. If you were black or Asian, you had to fit into this rigid strait-jacket; you had very few choices. You either went along with the well-hung-black or passive-Asian mythologies, or you withdrew into an exclusive and racially defined sub-culture.

In Britain, all this has worked in different ways. The black population is much smaller, and half of the Asian population will do its best to ignore questions of sexuality it doesn't like - I doubt if many Asians will be wending their way through the Mapplethorpe work at the Hayward. I came from New York to do degrees at Farnham and the Royal College of Art and found to my horror that attitudes prevailed that were pre-Stonewall. No mention was ever made of any gay practitioners or even a history of the gay sub-culture; it was left up to me to figure out a canon for myself (Tress, Mapplethorpe, Lynes and Minor White). Having discovered it, naturally I defended it to the full. Any visual references were surprisingly censored. In 1980 Sue Davies gave a lecture to my class and mentioned the Mapplethorpe work, but couldn't show any slides. When Sandy Nairne initially tried to bring the works over to the ICA they were disbarred by the customs officials who offered to burn them.

But there was a growing awareness of the pictures. In the 1980s, we discussed them in private, as black gays, and in public in *Ten.8*. I once wrote an article 'Desire and Black Men' which tried to pin-point the role of the black/Asian male as the subject of homosexual desire. Isaac Julien referenced the pictures in his film *Looking for Langston*. You can't begin a discussion of black gay representation without Mapplethorpe's work, and in that sense the canonisation has worked and the images now function as cultural icons. In Britain the response has been tremendous given the much smaller base we work from; witness the works of Fani-Kayode, Ajamu and Robert Taylor. It's hard to predict whether the Mapplethorpe pictures will continue to retain their relevance as a seminal, pivotal work about black gay men.

At the Hayward opening we overheard two young women discussing the fistfucking picture. They couldn't believe the photo was 'real' and were trying to convince themselves that it was a fake, a Photoshop phenomenon. Photography remains a tantalising medium - at once a metaphor for reality, a slice of life, an erotic artefact and a documentation. In another medium these images would have lost this appeal, 'are these people really doing what they appear to be doing?' What is annoying about the fistfucking picture is that it's become disproportionately well known to its artifice, that it tells us very little about the very real dangers to your health involved in this kind of activity, and that it tells us nothing about the participants, since its view is limited to orifice and forearm. Again, a fairly innocuous shot has become fashionable due to censorship. Back then you could go a club and see this for 'real', as you probably can today in London, which is enjoying a 1970s-style revival.

It's difficult to write about Mapplethorpe's work without taking into consideration his untimely death from AIDS. Sometimes seen as a metaphor for the 1970s: much of the work that we recognise now as part of the canon derives from that period and the emerging lesbian and gay sensibilities - a growing awareness that queer subject matter was being appropriated by queer practitioners for a queer audience. That the work is able to cross over into the mainstream at this point is a story of the intersection of a variety of interests; the anti-censorship lobby, the largely closeted gay section of the art world, the growing public face of homosexuality in the West and its attendant cultural politics.

1. For a discussion about race and Mapplethorpe's work see Kobena Mercer's essays in *Ten.8* and his book *Welcome to the Jungle*.

DERRICK CROSS, 1982

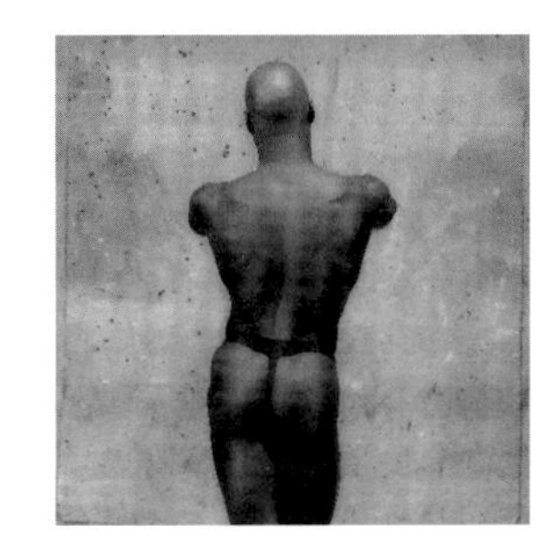

KEN MOODY, 1983

PATRICE, 1977

PORTFOLIO GALLERY 43 Candlemaker Row Edinburgh Scotland

RICHARD BILLINGHAM
Ray's a Laugh
23 November - 21 December 1996

SUNIL GUPTA
Trespass 3
11 January - 15 February 1997

CATHERINE YASS
Steel
22 February - 25 March 1997

ANTHONY HAUGHEY
The Edge of Europe
12 April - 17 May 1997

LYNN SILVERMAN
Interior Light
24 May - 21 June 1997

JOHN GOTO
The Framer's Collection
28 June - 26 July 1997

Sunil Gupta, Trespass 3

HELEN CHADWICK was one of the UK's most prominent and provocative visual artists whose primary medium was photography. A major catalogue has been published to accompany the exhibition of her final works, *Cameos* and *Unnatural Selection*, at Portfolio Gallery.

STILLED LIVES contains essays by Marina Warner, who surveys the artist's life's work, David Alan Mellor and Louisa Buck, and, in a unique insight into Helen Chadwick's art, an interview with Mark Haworth-Booth. This 68-page catalogue features 30 pages of exquisite colour photographs.

STILLED LIVES is available at £19.95 (plus £2 p+p) from Portfolio Gallery,
43 Candlemaker Row, Edinburgh, EH1 2QB, Scotland .

Tel 0131 220 1911 Fax 0131 226 4287

Sherrie Levine
South London Gallery

JOANNA LOWRY

AFTER DEGAS: 1, 1994
Sherrie Levine

The work of Sherrie Levine has been positioned critically as a quintessentially postmodern practice that questions traditional concepts of authorship, authenticity, value and high culture. In this context the idea of going to an exhibition of her work in a museum rather than viewing it in reproduction seemed to me to be interestingly perverse.

Once I had established that this was an exhibition of even more appropriations - photographs of reproductions of Impressionist and Post-Impressionist paintings culled from 1950s art books - was there anything more to be gained from actually going to see them? Of course, when I got there and I entered her subdued gallery of shadow images I had to admit that there was something to be gained, and something that reminded one of the complexity of the relationship between theory and practice.

Levine's work achieved a certain prominence in the early 1980s because, along with the work of artists like Richard Prince, Barbara Kruger, Cindy Sherman, etc., it provided a focus for a set of theoretical discussions about the nature of postmodernism and postmodernist art practice. Central to these discussions were the writings of Jean Baudrillard and the suggestion that postmodernity involved the dismantling of the necessary relationship between the sign and its referent, and consequently that we were trapped in a proliferating world of signs - a world of simulations. In the context of these debates, photography became positioned as *the* post-modern technology. These artists used it in a way that was quite antithetical to the endeavours of modernist art photography, building upon a conceptually based practice which privileged the mechanical, archival aspects of the technology above its use as a medium of artistic expression. Postmodernist theory produced a kind of protective shield around the work, a framework of concepts that held the photographic practice in place and imbued it with a kind of radical intention. It was as though the act of photographic reproduction itself was necessarily deconstructive.

This, of course, was a very particular reading of photography, and one which failed to totally account for the work itself. Levine's practice, which on the one hand was ostensibly committed to an undermining of originary meaning and a destabilisation of the sign, was on the other hand premised upon an engagement with the photograph as index, as a bearer of transparent evidence. This very specific kind of presence offered by the photograph, and its relative imperviousness to questions of intention, radical or otherwise, was not seen as so significant at the time.

Of course there were doubts expressed in some quarters, by critics like Hal Foster, about how radical Levine's practice really was, and about its disturbing tendency to reinscribe the discourse of artistic genius that it supposedly sought to dispossess. The question was whether Levine's practice had that disruptive force hailed by Walter Benjamin in his seminal essay 'The Work of Art in the Age of Mechanical Reproduction', a force that would make concepts like genius, mystery, and creativity obsolete, or whether she was actually, almost despite herself, contributing to Malraux's 'Imaginary Museum', in which technological reproduction simply served to disperse and reinforce a humanist cultural tradition. But it was not really recognised that this difficulty was perhaps to do with the profound ambivalence of the photographic image, itself split between its operation as a sign of displacement, deferral and simulation, and its origin as index, bearer of presence and loss.

It is this latter aspect of the photographic image that perhaps takes the theoretical centre stage today. The focus of our attention has shifted and photography seems to be important for what it implies for our notions of time, history and memory, of the interface between public knowledge and private imagination, of our own investment in the image. We are less interested in its feats of simulation than we are in its points of resistance - its failure to deliver. In the context of these discussions Levine's work takes on a different resonance.

The archive of images she presents to us - Cezanne's still-lives, Monet's views of Rouen Cathedral, Van Gogh's portraits, and Degas' ballet dancers and his *L' Absinthe* - repeated here twelve times - are all meticulously printed in black-and-white and perfectly framed. Each image is reduced to the same size and the same subdued grey tones, drained of the texture and colour that represented the painting's original promise of pleasure. This pleasure has itself been mechanically extracted in the final set of pictures in which colour images of Monet's paintings have been digitally analysed to produce a series of cool, poised, geometrical abstractions. Levine's art collection is a strangely sad and haunted place; the smooth textureless surfaces are devoid of expression. Yet the sense of the degradation of painting that these photographs represent is also paradoxically the source of their power. The real loss that they invoke reminds us of our imaginative investment in the image, of what we bring to it, of the longing that sustains it. Perhaps, looking at her work today, we sense that the language of deferral and displacement has itself been displaced by the language of loss. We find ourselves searching the image for something else, only to find that the photograph itself is somehow finite, while we had hoped for so much more.

The Visible and the Invisible: re-presenting the body in contemporary art and society
Euston, London

RUTH CHARITY

The workings of the human body and its relationship to the mind or soul have been the subject of our scrutiny for centuries, continually occupying the creative talents of writers, artists and philosophers. Today the subject seems to absorb us as never before - books and articles abound, and the art world is awash with exhibitions focusing on this theme. The exhibition *The Visible and the Invisible* curated by inIVA (The Institute of International Visual Arts), is yet another show that sets out to explore our complex contemporary responses to the body. However where it differs from many others is in its site-specific nature. Thirteen artists, eight of whom work with photography or video, have been selected to show either existing or newly commissioned work in four sites in the Euston area of London, each of which offers a specific context in which to consider the body – from the religious and spiritual to the medical and academic. It is in the way that these different venues have been utilised that both the strengths and weaknesses of the exhibition lie.

In St Pancras Church's still and peaceful interior four women artists show installation pieces - in the belfry, vestibule, crypt and grounds – their work hidden in dark corners, away from the gilt-edged splendours of the main body of the church, carving out their own spaces on the periphery of this male dominated preserve. Louise Bourgeois' *Cell* is reached by climbing a narrow spiral staircase to the bell tower. Entering the semi-gloom of the 'Ringing Chamber' you are confronted by larger-than-life, headless figures hanging from the rafters - a man, a woman and a couple clutched together in a desperate sexual embrace – their soft knitted bodies vulnerable and helpless. The deafening ring of the bells just above one's head and the steady tick of a metronome note the steady passing of time in this theatrical tableau - of hell? In the crypt, Jane Parker shows *Tomb*, a ghostly video of a female swimmer submerged in green and murky water, strangely at peace in her womb-like, self-contained limbo. At the base of a nearby stairwell, a light-box image of an ancient moss-covered tomb glows in dark, pointing up references to death and hidden histories. By fully exploiting the architecture of the church, both Bourgeois and Parker have created unsettling and claustrophobic meditations on the entrapment of death.

FLOOD, 1996
Jayne Parker

On a revolving billboard on Euston Road, Yoko Ono's *Celebration of Being Human*, carries the message – 'We are beautiful, we are fun, we are mammals without tails' – across an image of a bottom. Purportedly a message for peace, this one-liner is digested as quickly as the adverts for cigarettes and catfood which share its space.

The slick high-tech playground of the Wellcome Institute's *Science of Life* exhibition, is packed with interactive gizmos, buttons to press and computers to play with. Here, integrated amongst the permanent exhibits are art works that consider the physicality of the body and its health. Much of the work, such as Nancy Burson and David Kramlich's *Age Machine* which shows you what you may look like in 25 years time, is interactive, fusing seamlessly into its environment. The one piece that sits apart is Virginia Namarkoh's *Where Am I? 11*. This 'family tree' of Wellcome staff considers the institution as a whole, levelling its hierarchy by substituting adult photos with those of staff as babies.

Louise K Wilson's installation subverts its environment of didactic games by posing questions rather than offering solutions. *Possessed* requires you to lie on an analyst's couch and view scanned images of the brain, whilst a soothing male voice encourages you to relax and focus on your own body. It tells you your hand is being anaesthetised and you almost start to feel it numbing. But who is controlling who? Are you developing more acute awareness of your body or being induced by the machine to feel certain sensations?

At University College London artists consider the connection between mind and body, long the subject of academic debate. Entering Bruce Nauman's sound piece, an indecipherable but insistent voice gradually becomes clearer, until one can hear the words perfectly - 'Get Out of My Mind, Get Out of This Room'. Embarrassed at having entered someone's thoughts so unwelcomely, I left.

Maureen Connor's *Ensemble for Three Voices*, is perfectly suited to the intimate circular observatory in which it is installed. Three casts of a larynx and tongue are mounted on microphone stands, each accompanied by the sound of a child or woman laughing or crying. These red and gory images of flesh make one recoil in horror. Connor's eloquent work not only considers the mind/body divide but also makes us question why we find it difficult to come to terms with the mechanics of our bodies hidden beneath our protective layer of skin. Connor's installation, like the most powerful and memorable work in this exhibition, fully exploits the context of its site. By tailoring her piece to the genius of the place - its symbolism, function and architecture - art and context seem enmeshed, and the ideas embodied in her work are enhanced and invigorated. And like the most affecting work in the show, she makes us consider our bodies anew.

Erwin Blumenfeld: A Fetish for Beauty
Barbican Gallery, London

AMANDA HOPKINSON

UNTITLED NUDE, NEW YORK, c.1948
Erwin Blumenfeld

From low Dada into high fashion, from frenesis to fetishes, from the insanity of the War to end all wars to the elegance of post-World War II *Harpers Bazaar*, Erwin Blumenfeld stayed the course. That course took him from early years in a secluded, elegant, Jewish family (in explaining how, like many Central Europeans, he felt himself German rather than Jewish, he added that actually he was a Berliner rather than a German), through Amsterdam and Paris to New York, where he finally found his niche. And success: after repeated financial collapses and near-bankruptcies, he became according to the *New York Times* in 1941, 'one of the highest-paid photographers in the US' and, pace *Lilliput* only eight years' later, 'the world's most highly paid photo-grapher', retailing his cheapest shots for five hundred dollars apiece.

The transformation stands in stark opposition to the familiar argument telling us how magazines (or other media) must deliver what the audience wants. On the contrary, what Blumenfeld offered was entirely what concerned him and little his audiences had seen before. A key to his success is the immense seriousness and consistency with which he treated his life's work, refusing to discriminate against his earlier fascination with mixing media through the favoured artistic-isms of his times: from the tail-end of misty Impressionism to the sardonic satire of German Expressionism; from Paris-based Cubism to the heyday of Surrealism, there was little that escaped his magpie technique. And then there was Dada.

The loss of his teenage brother Heinz in the trenches caused him to create a collage around the absurdity of an 'autobiography' that opened, 'My parents died childless / I was never not-born / my brother fell in 1918 / I didn't fall for it myself' [my translation]. Dada was his natural metier, an assembled self-portrait sent to Tristan Tzara in 1921 signs off with *President-Dada-Chaplanist*, combining the vainglorious with the ludicrous, the vicious and the humorous. Self-portraiture expanded into a form of social commentary whereby foibles - prudery and narcissism - could be scrutinised. The reverse of the Rembrandt self-portrait he admired above all else. Then came the family, starting with his long-suffering wife Lena and then his three growing children, became heavily-directed camera fodder, grumbling that - unlike him - they were never permitted to invent themselves or devise their own portraits.

His childhood friend Paul Citroen was his one true collaborator, from their school-days on down the ensuing sixty years. Their first twenty years' mutual work (1919-39), covering Berlin, Amsterdam and Paris, was celebrated in joyful juxtaposition at the Photographers' Gallery, London, in 1993. From it, one would never have second-guessed a second career, going far beyond that experimentation with light and line, figure and form. The despairing game that was Dada and the clear lines of Bauhaus melded into a play on portraiture that involved solarisation and superimposition, multiple imagery and odd angles, the vertical frequently leading into the vertiginous.

Read backwards, however, all this was but a prelude to the heightened consciousness of the war years. Paradoxically, these signalled an end to the photomontages Erwin had been making of Hitler *à la* Heartfield - and like him, Blumenfeld mock-altered his name to Jan Bloomfield - superimposed onto a skull; with a swastika on this forehead or as a Minotaur; and his entry, from 1941, into an association with Carmel Snow at *Harpers* and then, via Beaton, with US *Vogue*. It was Cecil Beaton who persuaded him that, in 'a swinish world... when incompetent and dishonest politicians cannot be relied upon to prevent the bullies and the sadists' it was all the more necessary to find the artistic means of 'saving the world from barbarism'.

After four years of reducing his signature close-up of Jean Patois to the squiggle of an eyebrow and a lip and the dot of a pupil and a beauty mole, and elaborating the daring nature of his non-studio sets to include Lisa Fonssagrives genuinely perilously balancing on the Eiffel Tower or mounted across the bonnet of a Cadillac, Blumenfeld had achieved mass-celebrity status. Working now in colour (unafraid to put red on red on red as in the famous *Vogue* spread in 1954); autocratic as ever, but now affluent with it, he could well afford to row with any number of advertising directors and still retain portfolios for major cosmetic and jewellery clients.

While such images are part of our social history, it was Blumenfeld's artistry and not his art that was sought-after. While he claimed to smuggle his art in, 'Trojan horse' style, his artistic bulwark against the barbarians lay outside fashion, however inventively portrayed. Striking portraits of friends and famous names in the arts, from the ferocious intelligence of Eugene O'Neill to the soft profundity of Georges Roualt; from the gutteral film director Robert Flaherty to the pensive whimsy of Juliette Greco, he managed to mix the exigences of publicity shots with the power the eyes that, from the blow-up portraits on view at the Barbican, really do follow the viewer around the room. Alternatively, by dint of felicitous juxtaposition, there are the anticipations of Brandt's *Perspectives of Nudes* and a preoccupation with luminous ripples - of hair or sand; and avenue of poplars in Meudon or pillars in Rouen Cathedral; tyretracks in the mud or geological rifts in the Grand Canyon. Exquisite artistry and superlative black-and-white printing.

Mark Lewis: A Sense of the End and Two Impossible Films
Tramway, Glasgow

REBECCA COGGINS

Film is an increasingly fertile arena for artists, who recognise it as one of the shared cultural experiences of our age. In a feature entitled *Rosebud Anyone? - Artists' Favourite Films*, published some years ago by *Frieze* magazine, 35 artists and compiler Richard Flood named their favourite movies. The implication was not simply that the choices should illuminate each artist's oeuvre, but that by having also seen the film in question, the reader could claim a definitive experience in common with the likes of Cindy Sherman and Christian Boltanski.

Canadian artist Mark Lewis assumes that viewers of his works at Tramway are familiar with film, and it is film, rather than photography, that he presents in this exhibition. His images are not fixed, framed and proffered for leisurely inspection, but flow over the retina in a swift succession of what appear to be familiar film 'moments'. His avowed intention is not to question and subvert the nature of film itself - the subject of intervention by artists for several decades now - but to engage directly with the hegemony of the Hollywood-style movie. Lewis is wary of the narrative and therefore teleological structure of commercial cinema which presents things in a 'condition of process', leading to a finite end. He proposes an alternative form of cinema, a 'part cinema', made up of those incidental moments which threaten to escape resolution or explanation when it comes to the denouement, or 'distribution of prizes'.

The works presented at Tramway are very much 'part cinema'. Two consist of beginnings, one only of endings. Despite their

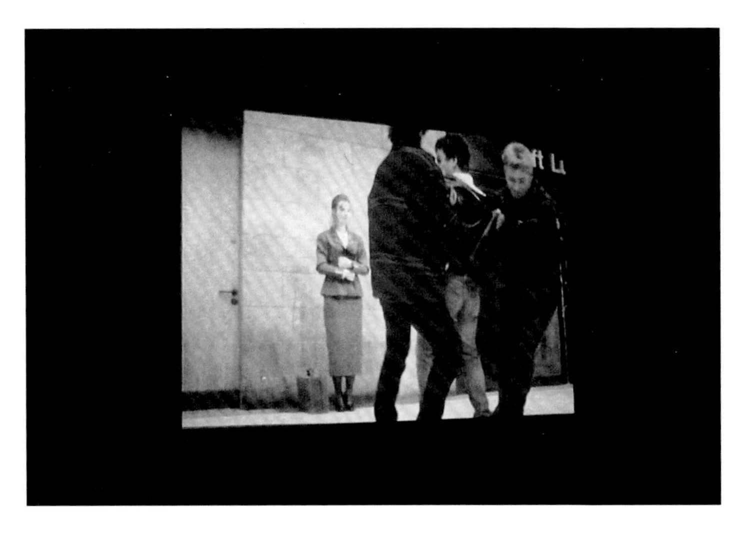

A SENSE OF THE END, 1996
Mark Lewis

fragmented nature, these works are in fact 'watchable', for Lewis exploits conventional cinematic devices to create drama and tension, punctured occasionally by humour. A young gangster, writhing in the dirt outside a warehouse, blood spilling out of his mouth, looks up at a tearful woman leaning over him. 'C'mon', he splutters, 'gi' me a kiss!'.

A Sense of the End is Lewis' latest work, filmed entirely on location in Glasgow. A succession of incidents - endings - filmed in a variety of film styles, is followed by a series of unrelated epilogues. A sense of fabrication and incongruity is underscored by the settings, which include the doorway of Tramway itself, not far from where the viewer is standing. A melodramatic sequence in Central Station was clearly filmed as normal people went about their business, for an old man turns in amazement to watch the jilted lover being manhandled away. His confusion seems to match that of the young gangster mentioned above, whose last words are an incredulous 'everybody's looking at me!'.

Lewis' two film beginnings (for dream projects never made - Samuel Goldwyn's definitive film on psychoanalysis and Eisenstein's cinematic version of Das Kapital) are scripted opening sequences reminiscent of the 'cinematic haiku' (Lewis) which precede most blockbuster movies. Using all the familiar devices, they succeed in both creating and deflating a sense of anticipation. Despite the list of credits, which include a Viennese production team, both are set in Lewis' native Vancouver.

The Story of Psychoanalysis follows the events of a day in a city park, the static camera lens obscured at both beginning and end by the cardboard box shelter of a tramp. Apparently insignificant events framed in this way become interdependent and by implication cyclical, continuing in endless repetition like screenings of the movie itself. In *Das Kapital*, as architectural plans are drawn up and construction work undertaken, the soundtrack becomes a lecture on Marx and Derrida in which Vancouver is identified as the 'terminal city', the conclusion of a line of thought which has travelled west from Europe to this peripheral point on the Pacific Rim. Vancouver's cinematic look is similar to that of Hong Kong, Singapore, Portland and Seattle, and, like these cities, it is a locus of what Lewis calls 'Capital *now*'. It is under a perpetual process of construction, as traces of the past - of history and identity - are erased and built over. As Lewis points out, Vancouver could double for many modern cities and has done so cinematically for several American ones. Unlike Glasgow, however, whose unmistakable identity permeates *A Sense of the End*, it has not yet played itself.

1. *Rosebud, Anyone? Artists' Favourite Films* by Richard Flood; *Frieze International Art Magazine*; Issue 9; March/April 1993.

SUBSCRIBE TO PORTFOLIO THE CATALOGUE OF CONTEMPORARY PHOTOGRAPHY IN BRITAIN

Ensure that you are kept informed of the most innovative photographic art being produced in the United Kingdom. Your support in the form of an annual subscription guarantees that this income goes directly into the publication, enabling us to continue to invest in the people creating a dynamic photographic culture. Complete and return the subscription form below with your cheque or credit card details.

SUBSCRIPTION RATES ARE AVAILABLE FOR 4 AND 2 ISSUES (JUNE AND DECEMBER)

United Kingdom Individuals £27 for 4 issues / £15 for 2 issues, Institutions £45 for 4 issues / £25 for 2 issues

Europe £45 for 4 issues / £25 for 2 issues **Worldwide** (Airmail) £55 for 4 issues / £30 for 2 issues

BACK ISSUES

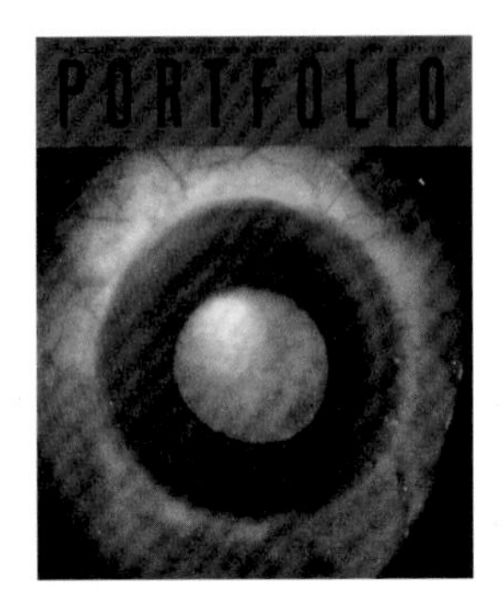

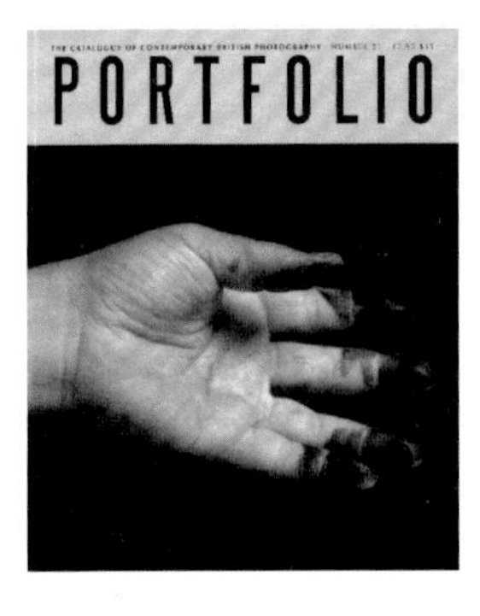

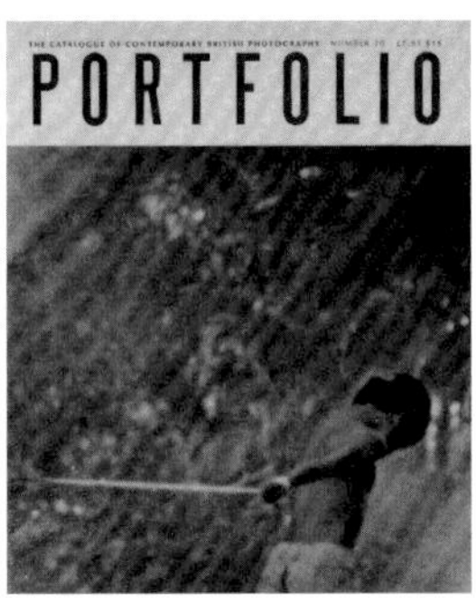

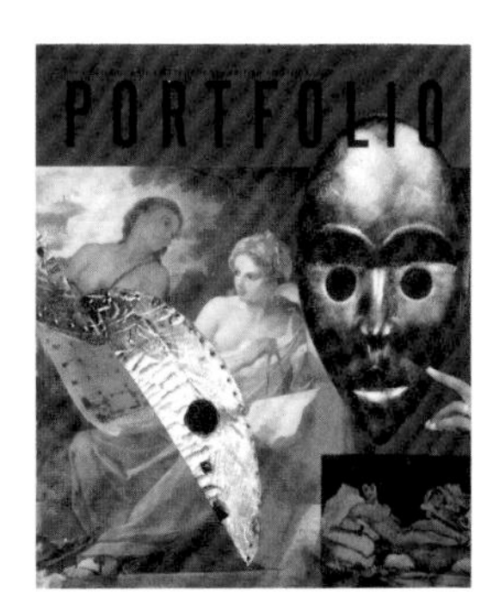

NUMBER 23	NUMBER 22	NUMBER 21	NUMBER 20	NUMBER 19
Helen Chadwick	Paul Graham	Andres Serrano	Yve Lomax	Maud Sulter
Jeff Wall	Joel-Peter Witkin	Helen Chadwick	Thomas Joshua Cooper	Karen Knorr
Orlan	Pavel Büchler	Hannah Collins	Mari Mahr	Boyd Webb
Susan Hiller	Martin Parr	Andrea Fisher	David Hiscock	Susan Trangmar
Keith Piper	Helen Sear	Olivier Richon	Lynn Silverman	Calum Angus Mackay
Liz Rideal	Allan Sekula	Roger Palmer	David Williams	John Stathatos
Katrina Lithgow	Wendy McMurdo	Catherine Yass	Roddy Buchanan	Anne Elliott
Clement Cooper	Lucinda Devlin	Zarina Bhimji	Lesley Punton	Catriona Grant

A set of back issues Numbers 1 to 18 (40 page A4 format) is available for £60 (UK) £65 (Europe and Worldwide).
For a complete list of back issues, see form below.

PORTFOLIO THE CATALOGUE OF CONTEMPORARY PHOTOGRAPHY IN BRITAIN

- ☐ Please start my subscription to PORTFOLIO with Number 25 *(June 1997)*
- ☐ Please send me back issue numbers *(please indicate)* ....
  Numbers 1-18 @ £3.50 (UK and Europe) £4.50 (Worldwide); Numbers 19, 20, 21, 22 & 23 @ £9.50 (UK and Europe) £12.50 (Worldwide)
- ☐ Please send me a set of back issues (Numbers 1 - 18) at £60 (UK) £65 (Europe and Worldwide)
- ☐ Please send me a free list of all back issues

I enclose a (Sterling) cheque
(made payable to PORTFOLIO) for £ ....

Or debit my Access/Visa/Mastercard (delete as applicable)

Name .... Expiry Date ....

Address ....

.... Postcode ....

Signed ....

Return to PORTFOLIO, 43 Candlemaker Row, Edinburgh, EH1 2QB Scotland UK Tel (44) 0131 220 1911 Fax (44) 0131 226 4287